THREE SOMEBODIES
PLAYS ABOUT NOTORIOUS DISSIDENTS

S.C.U.M. | ART WAS HERE | JACK THE RAPPER

BY

KAT GEORGES

THREE ROOMS PRESS

NEW YORK CITY

ISBN: 978-1-941110-54-6 (Trade Paperback)
ISBN: 978-1-941110-55-3 (Ebook)
Library of Congress Control Number: 2017960408

TRP-063

COVER AND BOOK DESIGN:
KG Design International
www.katgeorges.com

PUBLISHED BY:
Three Rooms Press, New York, NY
www.threeroomspress.com

DISTRIBUTED BY:
PGW/Ingram
www.pgw.com

To Peter Carlaftes

INTRODUCTION

IN SAN FRANCISCO FOR MOST of the 1990s, poet-playwright-actor Peter Carlaftes and I ran the small—but definitely fierce—theater company known as Marilyn Monroe Memorial Theater. We wrote, cast, and directed more than twenty-five plays. Between plays, we produced and presented numerous one-night-only events featuring poetry, film, sketch comedy, and Dada performance. The mission of the company was to present "demolished texts, deconstructed classics, and new works." We were entirely self-funded, disdaining the tendency for granting foundations to fund art that fit a certain profile. Ours did not. While our art was critically-acclaimed, we used the theater to explore ideas of rebellion and passion without restriction. As Peter likes to say, "We had no kitchen. The stage was our stove." Indeed, it was.

The plays cooked up in *Three Somebodies* were all inspired by notorious dissidents, people who shook up the world—for better or worse. Shakespeare had his kings and princes. I chose royalty of the infamous variety: Valerie Solanas, author of *The S.C.U.M. Manifesto*, who famously shot Andy Warhol; Arthur Cravan—nephew of Oscar Wilde, wild child pugilist and poet—whose legendary antics preceded and influenced the Dada movement; Jack the Ripper as sculpted through the words of T. S. Eliot's poem "Rhapsody on a Windy Night." Each play received its world premiere at the Marilyn, and earned high critical praise. But while each play is inspired by a person, be forewarned: the plays herein are not at all standard "bio-dramas." We didn't do bio-dramas at the Marilyn. These are stripped down, twisted, juxtaposed, hard-bent works of intensity designed to bring to life a three-dimensional portrait of each of the subjects, and to examine their particular personas from the inside out. The subjects of these three plays refused to be handcuffed by linear drama so they roar to life in twists and shouts, psychedelic tremors, and whirlwind ebullience.

So take your seatbelt off and get into the groove. Catch the waves, hug the curves, and take a ride you won't soon forget.

—*Kat Georges*

CONTENTS

THREE SOMEBODIES

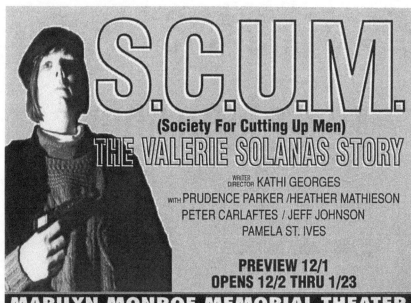

S.C.U.M.

The Valerie Solanas Story

Dedicated to
dominant, secure, self-confident,
nasty, violent, selfish, independent,
proud, thrill-seeking, free-wheeling,
arrogant females everywhere.

PRODUCTION NOTES:

I was introduced to Valerie Solanas' infamous work, *The S.C.U.M. Manifesto*, in the early 1990s and was consumed by the comic brilliance of her writing. How could this oddball genius succumb to shooting (and almost killing) pop art superstar Andy Warhol on June 3, 1968? Was she using him as the starting point of her mission to rid the world of men? Research led to the discovery that one of Solanas' main motivations for attacking Warhol was that he had allegedly promised to produce her original play, cleverly titled, *Up Your Ass*. On learning this, I immediately decided that she would be a great character for a play.

After shooting Warhol, Solanas was indicted and by August was sent to a mental hospital while awaiting trial. Somehow, for three days around Christmas of that year, she was let out of the hospital on bail (apparently paid for by an anonymous rich man). Warhol spent those three days riding around Manhattan in a limo and refusing to get out.

I started by determining that the play would be set in a party hosted at The Factory, and would be filled with Warhol superstars, all waiting for Warhol to show up. Instead, they get Valerie—and her mother—and all hell breaks loose.

I wrote and rewrote the play several times, but I wasn't satisfied. It didn't capture the madness of the era: the chaos, the crazed drug-infused sparkle, the breaking of all standards of the past. In frustration, I ripped up the first scene, ready to start writing again. But something happened. I glanced at the ripped up pages and started repositioning the pieces. Characters' dialogue was broken up and rearranged. It no longer made *linear* sense, but it had the energy I needed. I screamed and grabbed a pair of scissors and cut every page of the script into strips, cut monologues into pieces, grabbed some tape and fastened things together in a new order. It worked on the page. On the stage it was one of our most successful productions, reprised twice during our years at the Marilyn.

—*K. G.*

S.C.U.M.:
THE VALERIE SOLANAS STORY

CHARACTERS:

DOROTHY: *Valerie's mother; I would do anything for her*
VIVIAN: *Make me like death, like heroin*
GOLEM: *To be in love / is to love the beloved / just as he is*
BERNARD: *In their faces, I see hope*
VALERIE: *Don't struggle or kick or raise a fuss*

SETTING:

A party at Andy Warhol's Factory loft, furnished with a couch with a small table near it. A lamp on or near the table. A 16mm movie projector, three TVs, a small triangular raised area in a corner with a projection screen in pulled down front of it. Various art objects around the room, including the stump of a tree, painted fluorescent colors. Walls are filled with silk-screened square prints of Andy Warhol's Marilyn Monroe series.

It is early evening on the day of VALERIE'S *release on bail from jail, just over six months since she shot Andy Warhol. December 1968.*

As the audience enters the theater, they are accosted on the street by VALERIE *dressed in old jeans, a sweater, a cap ,and pea coat who wants them to purchase her writing. Fifty cents for women; a dollar for men.*

Inside, the SOUND *of Percy Faith's "Theme from a Summer Place" plays over and over again, fading with house* LIGHTS *to silence.*

Just after music fades, VALERIE *enters the theater and can be heard arguing with usher/house manager about being allowed to be let in. She finally convinces usher/house manager she will behave and will stand in the back.*

In BLACKOUT, DOROTHY *enters and crosses slowly with a creaky walker to a small table with lamp and couch. Turns on table lamp as she sits.*

DOROTHY: She has a terrific sense of humor. My life was not in vain. The day Valerie shot Andy Warhol, my husband, her father, called me drunk and said, "Look what your little slut did! If I had stuck around, I would have taught her how to behave."

I think he was right.

The Rolling Stones' "2000 Light Years From Home" rises as DOROTHY *speaks.* LIGHTS *rise as* VIVIAN *enters, talking fast and loud, carrying a police baton.* SOUND *of people at a party, over ongoing musical track of hip New York 1960s rock during course of the play.*

Once VIVIAN *enters,* VALERIE *begins whispering into audience members' ears occasional ad lib commentary on the action on the stage.*

VIVIAN: I can't believe it. I'm on my way over here tonight. And there's all these hippies protesting the war—from San Francisco or Hoboken or something—waving signs—whatever. Some Black Panther or something on a box just saying "Right on!" You know, some kind of righteous thing—and everyone's fist is in the air— And then it's like pandemonium! Cops. Tear gas. People flying. Cops cracking heads, knocking them on the ground. . . And I'm floating through . . . in slow motion. . . And then some cop is about to smash some hippy with his club. His club is back over his head—and I just reach up and grab it from him . . . and then walk away! See—here it is! I think it might look good as a . . . you know—neck tie or something funky.

Hands reach in from Offstage and grab police baton out of VIVIAN'S *hands. She stares for a moment at the spot where the club used to be, then crosses to* DOROTHY.

VIVIAN: So you're Valerie's mom. I can't believe . . . I mean, she's lucky to be out of jail.

DOROTHY: Hmm?

VIVIAN: It's almost ten. Valerie should be here by now. The party is going to start happening soon. I hope she's all right.

DOROTHY: She'll be here. Did you know her?

VIVIAN: Everybody knew Valerie. We used to make fun of her. S.C.U.M.? What's that? A drug? A virus? Oh . . . Society for Cutting Up Men. Oh, yeah—right—whatever. I bought *The S.C.U.M. Manifesto* just because she wouldn't leave me alone. One dollar. Two dollars for men. She always looked so pissed off at the world. I think she needed more vitamins. Or a poke of something. Some people went out of their way to avoid her, but they were just afraid because, unlike the rest of the world, she knew what she wanted. I think that's why we sort of got along.

Pause.

VIVIAN: Do you think she's ready to come back out?

DOROTHY: She said she has no regrets.

VIVIAN: Does she remember what it's like . . . out here?

DOROTHY: Do you mean will she do it again? She said no, she's over it now.

VIVIAN: The scene is still here, it will always be here. She was always beyond it anyway. A permanent feature of the world beyond. Always in the same clothing: the same old jeans and sweater, and the cap sitting straight on the top of her head. And her face . . . always the same expression frozen on her face. Never a smile.

DOROTHY: She didn't want to smile. She wasn't a "smiler."

DOROTHY *and* VIVIAN *speak the following speeches simultaneously.*

DOROTHY: Valerie was a . . . special . . . child. She was at the top of her class in grade school, and a good athlete, too. She especially loved to play baseball . . . she was an excellent batter, always hitting one home run after another.

At home, she loved to read everything, from the Bible to *Alice in Wonderland.* She read the newspaper to her father and me at the dinner table. I'll never forget when she read the news about Pearl Harbor, about how the Japs bombed America . . . in the innocent voice of a child . . . she didn't have any idea of the tragedy she was reading. It gives me goose pimples just to remember. That night, I couldn't stop crying.

VIVIAN: Anyway—Last night—you wouldn't believe last night. Insane. We went out to eat first. I wasn't too hungry so I just ordered dessert. Lemon meringue pie. I just ate the meringue. I didn't like the color of the lemon. Too yellow—it was too much of that fake color stuff—like a bad hair dye. The meringue was okay. Toasted on top. Egg whites . . .

So before that I met Jasmine over at her place. She was asleep, of course. I had to ring the doorbell in a really nervous way—she knows my ring—it's like "zzz-zzz, zzz-zzz, zz." She answered it. "Is that you, Vivian?" I said, "Yes, open up." She let me in. Her place was a mess, like, she had some people over the night before and a couple of them were still lying around.

I just vacuumed around them like they were small sofas or something. Put the trash in a bag, threw it out. She was in a terrible mood. She'd been doing barbiturates, so I gave her some amphetamine and then fixed her breakfast—a crouton. She put the A in her coffee and ate. And then she was a lot better.

VIVIAN *reaches into her purse, pulls out a box, opens it, pulls from it a smaller box, opens it, pulls from it a tiny bag, pulls from it two small pills, examines them closely, swallows one, replaces the other and puts everything back very neatly with extreme fastidiousness.*

DOROTHY *pulls a dark wool pageboy cap from her purse, stares an it, then sticks it on top of her head crooked and sits stone-faced; a reincarnation of her daughter,* VALERIE.

DOROTHY: She was so sweet, always offering to wash up the dishes after dinner, or mop up the floors on the weekend. Her father made a big production out of giving her a nickel when she did the weekend chores without being asked. After dinner on Sundays? . . .

Valerie would start cleaning up, and he'd say, "Hold it there, little lady. Before you lift another dirty plate, I have a few words to say to you." And she would sit down giggling.

Then he'd say, "Little princess, because you are such a good girl, Daddy wants you to have this small token of his appreciation."

SOUND *Music up slightly.*

Enter GOLEM.

As DOROTHY *speaks, he plugs in a movie projector in the corner.*

VIVIAN *walks around, stretching, starts speaking halfway through* DOROTHY'S *next speech. She is increasingly frantic and trying desperately to stay under control.*

DOROTHY: She took the nickel from him and then gave him the biggest hug her little arms could give. After looking at that nickel for a second, she'd shove it into her pocketbook and immediately start cleaning up the dishes.

8

One day, her father got drunk and ran out of money. He tore apart the whole house until he found Valerie's little pocketbook and emptied it out on the table in front of her.

She screamed, "Daddy, you said that money was mine!" And he screamed and slapped her across the face and sent her flying.

I tried to stop him and he hit me with his fist and knocked out one of my teeth.

He counted all the money—there was only $1.50—but it was all the money she had. He gathered it up and walked out the front door, leaving the empty pocketbook on the table.

VIVIAN: She was always sort of outside the scene. She had her own agenda. But she was always around. I was walking one afternoon on a beautiful day on methedrine, cocaine, vitamins, and . . . I forget . . . something else . . . and, anyway, I was thinking about a painting I was going to do of the Pope, naked in a supermarket, and some plans for building a plastic Kabuki house and starting my own clothing line made from empty coke cans . . . and Andy, of course.

And just at that moment, Valerie walked up to me and started asking me, "Why do you let Andy exploit you?" And I realized, what she meant wasn't Andy, really, but all men, and she was right. Andy exploited women, just like other men.

DOROTHY *begins singing.*

VIVIAN: Even though he always gave them the option. Women would come up to him and say, "Can I be in your movie?" and he'd say, "Yes, if you take your shirt off." And they'd think about it for, like, two seconds, these fallen society women looking for kicks, and they'd show up the next day and take their shirt off.

While VIVIAN *rants,* GOLEM *starts projector. During* VIVIAN's *previous speech,* DOROTHY, *wearing the cap, begins to dance and sing in the beam from the projector. Movie is a black-and-white 16mm film of* VIVIAN *and* GOLEM *kissing.*

DOROTHY: *(sings) I want to be in the movies / I want to be the way you are / I'll do anything you want / Just make me a Super Star!*

GOLEM *squats and frames his hands around* DOROTHY *looking for perfect camera angle.*

GOLEM: *(poetically)* The blue light of her eyes. . . the raven hair of youth hides under silver . . . the smile breaks from years . . . inside, a heart lies . . . another heart speaks only truths.

Pause. GOLEM *stands.*

GOLEM: I could just as soon be living a lie, where everything is made up, including you.

GOLEM *turns off projector. Exit* GOLEM.

DOROTHY *becomes suddenly exhausted and stumbles back to her couch. She sits just as* VIVIAN *finishes speaking previous speech.* VIVIAN *sits near* DOROTHY.

DOROTHY: Is he still the same? This . . . Andy Warhol?

VIVIAN: Andy's changed. Since Valerie shot him he put a lock on his front door, everyone's got to be scrutinized before they come in. All those crazy people who used to just wander in and hang out . . . those disillusioned lunatics flashing weird eyes and nowhere minds were his sole source of inspiration. Now, he's just a ghost, a walking ghost.

VIVIAN *sits up sharply, with a sudden burst of energy, with a flash of anger from a drug-magnified thought.*

VIVIAN: Somebody should have rammed an icepick up his ass a long time ago . . .

But . . .

Suddenly calm again. Who's got the time?

VIVIAN *digs around through her purse. Pulls out a mirror and begins applying mascara to her false eyelashes.*

VIVIAN: Yesterday, I needed a few cosmetics, so Jasmine and I went shopping. Ha! Shopping! They've got our pictures on all the registers, like, people to watch, for taking stuff.

We walk into Macy's, and Jasmine starts talking to the clerk, but it's too much of a hassle: I feel like I'm in the Academy Awards or something, with everybody watching me. I couldn't grab anything!

So we go over to Gimbel's and—wow!—it's the same scene. We are known in these places.

This time I start talking to the clerk about–I don't know—fucking Christmas sales being up or something . . .

Enter GOLEM *with a tray of salami. Sets it on table near couch that* DOROTHY *sits on. Turns on three TVs, which all play different 1960s era black-and-white underground movies.*

VIVIAN: And, I figure, Jasmine doesn't stand a chance of not being caught—we are known here—and then I see her walk out the door and so I leave saying, "Merry Christmas" or some bullshit to the chick behind the counter—she's Jewish—I don't give a shit—

and then I'm out the front door, I walk down the block, and there is Jasmine—big grin all over her face, and—check this out—she has mascara, three kinds of lipstick, Chanel No. 5, two sets of leotards, four sets of false eyelashes, and a gift set of eye shadow. The girl is incredible!

A couple of security guards near the front door see her showing me all the stuff and start getting weird, but we just give them a look of radiance . . . and they leave us alone!

VIVIAN *looks up, sees* GOLEM, *then looks away quickly back at* DOROTHY.

VIVIAN: Hey, look! It's Golem.

GOLEM: What are you doing here, Vivian? Thought you split for some commune in Vermont.

VIVIAN: I came back to meet Valerie. She's late.

GOLEM: Valerie Solanas? She's in jail.

VIVIAN: Some rich man no one knows bailed her out this morning.

GOLEM: Unbelievable! Valerie's back on the streets? Does Andy know?

DOROTHY: Don't worry, young man. She won't do it again.

GOLEM: How do you know?

DOROTHY: She told me.

GOLEM: And who are you?

VIVIAN: Oh, this is Val's mom.

GOLEM: Hmmmmm . . . The beautiful is that which we cannot wish to change. Unlike your daughter, you are beautiful.

She has taken a trip beyond the streets of this city. Elapsed into the turbulence. Good bye.

VIVIAN: You don't understand.

GOLEM *and* DOROTHY *start talking to each other as* VIVIAN *continues.*

VIVIAN: Talk about turbulence. Last night, the wind was not blowing anywhere. We all go out to eat, then hit up a couple parties, a couple clubs. The whole town is dead.

Someone says—it's the change of season? From what to what? I want to know. I mean, please . . . change of season? What does that mean? You wear a coat, you go out, you tip the limo driver an extra buck.

People just never want to inhabit the inside of themselves.

The inside . . .

. . . it's not something seasonal . . .

GOLEM: What I understand is love and beauty and life and death.

DOROTHY: I think that's exactly what we're talking about.

GOLEM *looks at* DOROTHY, *circles her. Takes a photo with a small inexpensive camera from the era. Moves in close.*

DOROTHY: I wish you wouldn't do that.

GOLEM: I'll ask next time.

Without asking, GOLEM *takes another photo.* DOROTHY *does not object.*

DOROTHY: Valerie said to meet her at the party. I've never been to this kind of party before. When I was young, parties were much different. We had structure. We played games. We invited people who liked each other and were good guests.

GOLEM: Nothing's changed. Don't worry. We'll have a good time.

GOLEM *moves to* DOROTHY'*s side, blows gently on her neck and whispers.*

GOLEM: On windy evenings there's a smell of moisture in the air. The smell her body had when it was young. Under all those clothes.

DOROTHY: That feels lovely. Like a warm island breeze.

GOLEM: Tonight, Dorothy, is a very special night. This is not just any party . . . but a very special party. A chance to remember what we strive to forget. A chance to hold onto a dream of happiness for moments at a time and to escape the petty world in which we live.

DOROTHY: You make me feel so young.

GOLEM: You are young. A young girl. Naïve in her beauty. Legs that move without knowledge.

GOLEM *kisses* DOROTHY'*s neck.*

GOLEM: Beautiful woman-girl. Let's dance.

GOLEM *helps* DOROTHY *stand without her walker.*

SOUND *Music rises, "Coconut Grove" by Loving Spoonful.*

GOLEM *and* DOROTHY *dance.* VIVIAN *paces. Bored and angry. Sits on couch. Fidgets.* VIVIAN *starts speaking to get* GOLEM*'s attention (unsuccessfully) as* DOROTHY *and* GOLEM *talk and dance.*

VIVIAN: Last night, everyone was so boring. I got bored. Okay, so what? I should have stayed home. Okay, right. But I had this urge, from the I Ching that I was needed out in the world last night.

So, okay. I go.

Jasmine and I and those guys are just cruising from party to party, thinking about having a good time, but no such luck. All the parties are full of a bunch of rich PR snobs.

They take one look at Jasmine and me, and they just want to throw us out. But they want the guys to stay, of course. Whatever. I'll never hang around with those gay boys again.

So we just tripped around, then finally ended up running into Randy. *(Looks around, expecting a reaction. Disappointed to find no one is listening to her.)*

DOROTHY: You know I used to dance so much with Val's father. To all the old songs. We were in love.

We met at a dance hall. Sam worked at a bank and he would always buy me jewelry. Then he'd say, "Okay, baby cakes, now that you look so pretty, let's go out, so I can show the world my girl—she's all mine!"

I loved to hear him say things like that. It made me feel special . . . to be desired by someone . . . to be wanted. I was sure that feeling was love.

GOLEM: To be in love . . . is to love the beloved . . . just as he is . . .

DOROTHY: That's beautiful.

GOLEM: Someday, I'll write a poem about it.

GOLEM *and* DOROTHY *dance some more, like two people in love.* VIVIAN *watches with growing antagonism, takes a different pill, then starts dancing herself as it kicks in.*

DOROTHY: Oh, I have to sit down for a bit.

GOLEM *leads* DOROTHY *to the couch, where, breathless, she sits.*

VIVIAN *moves in toward* GOLEM.

VIVIAN: Oh, Randy told me the funniest joke last night at Bob's opening . . . but I can only remember the punch line . . . what was it? . . . something like, "Oh, sorry . . . wrong number! . . .

VIVIAN *laughs loudly and uncontrollably.*

GOLEM *and* DOROTHY *ignore her, still talking to each other.*

GOLEM: I must leave . . .

DOROTHY: Where are you going?

GOLEM: Away! . . . Then . . . Back again!

GOLEM *exits, twirling.*

VIVIAN *dances.*

DOROTHY *taps her fingers and reminisces.*

DOROTHY: One night after we were married, Sam and I went out to the dance hall . . . the nightclub where we had met. This fellow there was looking at me. Sam had just bought me a new bracelet and I was wearing a very well-tailored satin dress that fit me to a T. This fellow just kept staring.

Well, after a while, I looked at him and smiled. And he smiled back.

Sam was just coming from the men's room and he saw us smiling at each other and he just went crazy.

He grabbed the man and threw him on the ground and started kicking his face, until a few of the other guys in the place pulled him off and threw him out.

I ran out to meet him, and as soon as I was out the door, he grabbed me and started shaking me and pulling my hair and slapping my face and screaming, "You slut, I can't trust you by yourself for a minute!"

We never went to that club again.

As DOROTHY *speaks,* VIVIAN *grows suddenly startled as if hearing a strange noise.*

VIVIAN: Wait, who's that?

VIVIAN *crosses to entry, looks out, comes back, bored.*

VIVIAN: Oh, it's no one. . .

GOLEM *and* BERNARD *enter. Begin talking from offstage.*

BERNARD: Where were you? When I tell you to be someplace at 9:30, I expect you to be there at 9:25! Got it?

GOLEM *begins trying to sell* BERNARD *on his movie idea.* BERNARD *listens with lack of obvious interest, crosses immediately to the salami table, picks up a piece of salami and delicately eats it, a nibble at a time.*

GOLEM: Okay—the first shot is an extreme close-up of . . . well, no one can tell exactly what it is, except that there are darks and lights and they are moving. Could be flesh. Could be water reflecting. Could be a petri dish experiment. No one knows . . .

We pull back, little by little, extremely slowly . . . slowly . . . slowly . . . and at some point . . . boom!—the screen goes to bright white and "America the Beautiful" begins to play, and we see that the bright white is the sky on a sunny day on the beach.

The camera pans down to a long shot of people on the beach, all happy and laying around, kids with pails and shovels and teenage girls laughing and looking at teenage boys. What could be more beautiful in America, right? Of course . . .

GOLEM *continues speaking as* VIVIAN *and* DOROTHY *start to converse.*

DOROTHY *can't stop staring at* BERNARD's *conservative appearance.*

BERNARD *focuses only on his own actions.*

VIVIAN *is bored by every glance at* BERNARD *and tries her best to rile him with sardonic remarks.*

VIVIAN: Valerie had a play. I liked the title. *Up Your Ass.*

DOROTHY: I think it sounds filthy.

VIVIAN: Andy said he was going to make a movie out of it. But he deceived her. He never gave her back the script.

DOROTHY: Maybe it wasn't very good.

VIVIAN: It doesn't matter.

DOROTHY: Of course it matters.

VIVIAN: No, what matters is—he went back on his word.

DOROTHY: Maybe he just changed his mind.

VIVIAN: He manipulates people!

DOROTHY: He didn't force her to give him the script.

VIVIAN: He's a goddamned liar! He said I was his next Superstar! And now he's got the transvestite instead of me! He lied!

DOROTHY: Lots of people lie. You don't try to kill them.

VIVIAN: You don't try. If someone fucks you over, then Valerie's right. . . . Just stick a gun in the asshole's face and boom!—one less asshole.

DOROTHY: Aren't you against killing? People are dying in Vietnam, on the streets, killing themselves. . . . You don't really think you could ever kill someone . . . do you?

VIVIAN: No one who fucks up my world deserves one single more breath.

DOROTHY: Have you ever killed?

VIVIAN: No. That's why Valerie is important. She tried . . . —

DOROTHY: She failed . . .

VIVIAN: She did not fail. We fail. Everyday. We just sit and dance and make these movies and art that are unconnected. Valerie at least connected.

DOROTHY: Attempted murder is not connecting.

VIVIAN: Sex and violence are the only connection we've got. Language is a thing of the past.

DOROTHY: You only say what you think I should hear.

VIVIAN: Nobody listens to words anymore.

DOROTHY: I'm listening.

VIVIAN: But not to me.

GOLEM *speaks this over* DOROTHY *and* VIVIAN's *previous conversation.*

GOLEM: So the song continues to play, and the camera zooms in on a group of young girls—the future of America, right? Suntanned, blond, pre-pubescent, wearing those cute little bathing suits. Skin exposed. They get up and walk over to the hamburger stand and buy hamburgers and one of them buys a milkshake.

The camera closes in on her, as though buying a milkshake is the most significant event in the world.

And as the camera holds on her, sucking up that thick, creamy milkshake, struggling to get it to come up through the straw, little cheeks straining and sucking—boom!—there's a flash to a scene of a man in leather with a whip. Flash! Back to the girl.

And then there's a series of these flashes between these leather scenes, and always back to the innocent young girl sucking on that little straw. And all the while "America the Beautiful" is playing, because this really is a beautiful country.

And then the music changes to some kind of carnival music. And the man who was in leather is now at the beach sucking on a milkshake and girl is in leather swinging the whip around.

And this is interspersed with pictures of a roller coaster, a skyscraper, a train, an airplane. Close-ups of twisted faces rushing off to work from the crowded subway. An empty easy chair. A mirror. A clock.

Then—flash!—a scene of a crowd of happy children running out of the front door of their school. So many happy children, they just keep coming and coming, we'll talk to central casting, get thousands. Never have so many happy children been seen anywhere in film history.

End of movie.

I call it . . . "Tan Lines."

Pause by all ONSTAGE.

Then VIVIAN *turns to* DOROTHY.

VIVIAN: So, what do you think . . . of Valerie's writing?

DOROTHY: I never read any of it.

MUSIC *continues, Velvet Underground's "Sunday Morning."*

BERNARD *looks at his watch,*

DOROTHY *looks at* GOLEM.

GOLEM *turns on projector, with weird psychedelia.*

VIVIAN *looks through her purse, finds another pill, eats it, then begins dancing in the beam of the projector.*

BERNARD *turns to* DOROTHY.

BERNARD: Do try the salami. It's exquisite.

DOROTHY: I'm not very hungry. I'm waiting for my daughter.

BERNARD: Yes, Golem mentioned you were Valerie's mother. She's a frightening creature.

DOROTHY: She wasn't always that way. She was so sweet, once . . .

BERNARD *and* DOROTHY *speak at the same time under the pretense of holding a true conversation. Exit* GOLEM. VIVIAN *continues to dance in projector's beam.*

BERNARD: . . . truly frightening. Not unlike the coyote, in many respects. No one understands such creatures.

Have you heard of Beuys? Joseph Beuys? His coyote piece was quite remarkable. Such vision! Here is a man, who knows the American *esprit* better than most Americans themselves. He saw the persecution of the coyote as an example of the American tendency to project his own sense of inferiority onto an object of hate or a minority. So he created a living art piece that focused entirely on the coyote. In fact, he wanted to see nothing of America during his trip other than the coyote.

DOROTHY: I don't think Valerie ever understood her father. He worked so hard. When the Depression hit Sam lost his job at the bank, and I started working here and there where I could . . . ironing shirts, selling cosmetics door to door . . . Sam finally got part-time work as a janitor . . . it killed him. Our dreams of buying a house fell to pieces. Valerie was born in the middle of this nightmare . . . I even thought about giving myself an abortion . . . But Sam would have killed me. We vowed that our child would never have to face the kind of hardships we faced. From the time she was born we taught important values like kindness, responsibility, and hard work. She was a strong-willed child. We tried.

BERNARD *and* DOROTHY *continue to speak at the same time.* VIVIAN *continues to dance.*

BERNARD: Here's what Beuys did: He arrived at JFK and was wrapped in felt, laid on a stretcher, and driven by ambulance to the gallery. There, he went into a cage with his coyote for two weeks. Each day, he stacked the latest issue of the Wall Street Journal in two piles of twenty-five copies each. He wore brown gloves, had a flashlight with him, and leaned on a walking stick. Gradually, he set out to get close to the coyote.

DOROTHY: Divorce is never easy, especially for a child. Sam started drinking . . . the yelling lasted till dawn . . . things broke . . . he left. I thought I could raise Valerie by myself. I had a little savings. I worked part time. For years, we were best friends. And suddenly . . . I don't know . . . hormones, drugs, sex, something happened to her. One day she was my daughter . . . the next day, I didn't want anyone to know we had ever been close.

While DOROTHY *and* BERNARD *are "conversing," enter* GOLEM.

VIVIAN *dances over to him and erotically attempts to turn him on.*

VIVIAN: Aren't you going to dance tonight?

GOLEM: Later.

VIVIAN: You're so beautiful . . .

GOLEM: The beauty in you is apples is grapes is desperate in its attempt to be visible as you hide your face behind hands with outstretched fingers and wade in water too shallow to swim in.

VIVIAN: What do you mean?

GOLEM: We'll have a reason to remember each other . . . but not now.

VIVIAN *stops dancing, disappointed, pouts.*

GOLEM *crosses away from* VIVIAN *and starts snapping flash pictures of everything but her on the stage.*

VIVIAN: Where's Valerie?

GOLEM: I see things from behind the camera lens. Just aim and shoot. I edit vision. I focus on one tiny part of the big blur to give it the importance lost in the whirl of society.

A poet is like a cameraman. Aim and shoot. Enter the world of voyeurism and risk. Reality is, after all, just that which is seen, just as long as it is, or can be, seen. Reality is a movie, the iris of our eye focusing onto the film of our mind, as we record moments to be edited and replayed to an ever-changing audience whose only constant member is . . . ourself.

BERNARD *and* DOROTHY *continue to speak at the same time.*

BERNARD: Beuys wrapped himself in felt, leaving only the stick protruding, and lay down on the floor. A sculpture. Brilliant. He stacked other pieces of felt into a pile from which the flashlight shone. He talked to the coyote and encouraged him to tug at the felt strips and tear them.

Then the situation was reversed: the coyote curled up on the felt, and Beuys lay down on the coyote's straw. From time to time, Beuys made "music" with a triangle, which he wore suspended around his neck. Then the taped sounds of turbines broke the silence.

Three days and nights later, the two were used to each other. Beuys said goodbye to Little John, hugging him gently. He scattered the straw in the room in which he had lived with the animal. Once more, Beuys was wrapped in felt, laid on a stretcher, and taken to JFK airport in an ambulance. And so he left New York, having seen nothing of the city beyond the room with the coyote.

DOROTHY: Valerie got involved with a sailor. She was only fifteen . . . he was a big brute with a car. I'm sure that's what attracted her the most. I handed him Valerie's bag at a hamburger stand . . . she didn't have the guts to tell me goodbye. She was too weak. A whimpering, sulking, mindless coward, just another stupid girl. She really hasn't changed much . . .

I would do anything for her . . .

VIVIAN *speaks, overlapping* BERNARD *and* DOROTHY.

VIVIAN: My mother came to visit me here. She said she wanted to meet my friends. I helped her put on her makeup . . . We went to a party . . . She flipped out! The lights, the smells, the music, the people. There's a table with some food on it—some cheese and fruit and salami, so I tell her, "Just stay here, Mom—I'll be right back." I get lost in some dancing, and Golem is doing his whip dance and next thing I know, two hours have gone by, and I'm saying, "I left my mom at the salami table—two hours ago!" So I go back. And she's right where I left her. And she's talking with Andy Warhol like they're best friends or something. I mean, for the two of them, no one else exists! I've never seen her that happy.

DOROTHY: Is there anything to eat here? I'm starving!

VIVIAN: There's always salami—over there!

VIVIAN *starts laughing hard, and continues laughing, staring at herself in a compact mirror, looking in her purse for another pill, and laughing some more. Spastic, then controlled.*

GOLEM *changes reels on the projector.*

BERNARD *elucidates further on Beuys, assuming everyone is listening to him. Which they aren't.*

BERNARD: I was able to observe Beuys' ritual—you can't possibly demean it by calling it a "performance"—and I must say, it was stunning. This man, unarmed, willingly climbed into an area where he could be attacked—killed by a wild beast. He became the animal we see in zoos. He illuminated the animal in us all, and the baseness of what we call civilization.

Though I must say, the straw was a bit much. And the felt—he chose, for some reason, a kind of forest green, a bit of an easy choice, if you ask me. Lavender would have added such a nice dimension.

GOLEM *finishes changing reels on project. Looks at* BERNARD, *who asks him—*

BERNARD: Don't you agree?

GOLEM *crosses to small stage in corner, raises projection screens, strips off his shirt to a leather chest harness, strikes a pose.*

GOLEM: And now, I am ready to dance.

VIVIAN: With me?

GOLEM: Later. Watch.

VIVIAN: Now?

DOROTHY: Now?

BERNARD: Now . . . ?

GOLEM: Now.

MUSIC *cue: Velvet Underground's "Venus in Furs."*

LIGHT *off except* STROBE LIGHT *and* BLACK LIGHT. PROJECTOR *starts with psychedelic arty film, aimed toward stage on which* GOLEM *dances.*

GOLEM *dances like a dominatrix with a florescent whip.* DOROTHY *and* VIVIAN *watch him with intense interest.* BERNARD *watches him, loses interest quickly and turns his back to watch one of the televisions instead.*

DOROTHY: He's very good.

VIVIAN: He's a master of the dance. I wish . . . I never . . . had to see him dance again.

DOROTHY: He seems like such a nice man. He reminds me of Valerie's father in a way. Strong, clever . . . good dancer.

VIVIAN: I can't watch him . . .

DOROTHY: Why not?

VIVIAN: He mesmerizes me . . . When I see him dance, I see the dance of time.

VIVIAN *becomes a snake, begins sidewinding sexily toward* GOLEM *on the stage. She speaks in a trance.*

VIVIAN: I become a snake, crawling through an endless sea of broken glass and rusted plastic. I try to hold on, but the rope has frayed with the fire of presence. Falling into flames of desire . . . I lose . . . my sense . . . of incense . . .

DOROTHY *loses interest, eats salami, and speaks to* BERNARD.

DOROTHY: Great salami. I love good food . . . It makes me forget . . .

BERNARD: Oh, I had a fabulous lunch today at the de Menil Foundation with Nelson. He had some rather unusual ideas for a retrospective of leaf rubbings from the Galapagos Islands. Apparently, a tenth of the trees in the Galapagos do not grow anywhere else in the world. And really—why should they?

BERNARD *laughs heartily.*

BERNARD: Very interesting. Nelson figured that we could take the de Menil's jet down there, pluck a few leaves, fly back, and have Jasper and-or Andy and-or Robert each take a turn with a rubbing. "Perfect," I told Nelson, as we were sipping our digestifs. I indicated that I would speak to Dominique immediately. Leaf rubbings by today's most significant artists. Brilliant.

VIVIAN *grows increasingly wide-eyed, dancing in circles in front of the stage.*

VIVIAN: Speed is the ultimate all-time high. That first rush . . . wow! . . . Just that burning serum, the ultimate sense of perfection . . . that twenty-four-hour climax . . . that can go on for days . . .

SOUND *cue: Change* MUSIC *to Velvet Underground's "Femme Fatale."*

LIGHT *cue: Increasingly weird.*

GOLEM *dances with phosphorescent glow tape.* VIVIAN *crawls up to the stage. They dance.*

DOROTHY: . . . and remember a simpler time. I used to tuck Valerie in every night with a fairy tale. She loved to hear that song Little Red Riding Hood sang as she was skipping through the forest.
Who's afraid of the big, bad wolf?
The big, bad wolf
The big, bad wolf?

I must have sung it to her a hundred times. And she would always look up at me and say, "Mommy, are you afraid of the Big Bad Wolf?"

And I would think about all the bills that were due and the rent and her father showing up every once in a while drunk and violent, and how I had no idea if I was going to be able to survive even one more day in this world.

And I would look back into her big, innocent eyes, that wanted only the truth.

And I would hide all my fear and tell her, "Valerie, honey, I know the Big Bad Wolf. I know him very well. And I am not afraid for one second. He can't scare me."

From the back of audience, where she has been commenting every so often on the action on stage, VALERIE *suddenly gets extremely upset at her mother, and shouts.*

VALERIE: Liar!

VALERIE *rushes onto the stage. During her next comment, all action stops.*

VALERIE: LIFE in this society being, at best, an utter bore and no aspect of society being at all relevant to women, there remains to civic-minded, responsible, thrill-seeking females only to over-throw the government, eliminate the money system, institute complete automation, and destroy the male sex.

DOROTHY: You're too late, Valerie.

MUSIC *starts again.* GOLEM *and* VIVIAN *resume dancing, though both with occasional worried glances at* VALERIE.

VALERIE: I'm right on time. There is no place left for men in this world. Not if we are to avoid getting the whole marble blown to smithereens by a power-crazed psycho who is pissed off one day because his wife won't suck him off before his morning press conference from the Oval Office. Men are a walking disease, cured only through elimination. Castration alone is not the answer.

DOROTHY: What do you mean?

VALERIE: The male has a negative Midas touch—everything he touches turns to shit. Completely egocentric, trapped inside himself, incapable of empathizing or identifying with others, incapable of love, friendship, affection, or tenderness, a half-dead, unresponsive lump, he is at best an utter bore, an inoffensive blob.

VALERIE *paces restlessly, like a* COYOTE.

BERNARD *elucidates, alternately addressing* GOLEM *and* VIVIAN, DOROTHY, *and* VALERIE, *all with a clear sense of precision, to which no one pays any attention. All start speaking at simultaneously.*

GOLEM *and* VIVIAN *continue to dance, getting closer and more erotic, and speak/sing.*

BERNARD: My father loved the Galapagos, as a young adventurous troubadour. But the Galapagos today? Leaf rubbings by abstract expressionists and pop artists? Yes, well—old Nelson is affable enough, but somebody must have slipped something in his morning coffee. Perhaps I'll send him a bottle of twenty-five-year-old Glen Farclas to cheer him up in his demise.

VIVIAN: I think my favorite sensation of all is the sense of sight. I mean—let the hippies have all that touchie-feelie stuff. And taste is okay, but I don't really like to eat much. What's left? Sight . . . beautiful sight. Open your eyes and just look at your thumb—it's as if you're seeing another world. All those ridges are like highways that lead to other highways that lead to other highways that lead to anywhere you want.

Stop looking at your thumb and step outside and the whole world is just there and it looks different every second. The light changes, the people change, it's all action, action, action, and a blur of color and motion.

BERNARD: It is not the Nelson Rockefellers of this world that are going to be creating the masterpieces that last into the 21st century and beyond. There are no new masterpieces—Artaud. Except for one or two deKoonings, a couple of Pollacks, a Rauschenberg or three, several of Warhol's silkscreens. Near-genius. No, perhaps not so near.

Picasso was the last great master and even the majority of his work is not up to the level of Guernica. I don't care one iota for masterpieces anyway. Let the nouveau riche think in terms of masterpieces. Helps expand the marketplace for art and increases the value of one or two modern painters, preferably ones I represent.

GOLEM: Is the person worth the inspiration? Am I worth the time it takes to absorb it all, throw it all out? and . . . who is . . . transformed?

VALERIE: The male's greatest need is to be guided, sheltered, protected and admired by Mama (men expect women to adore what men shrink from in horror—themselves) and, being completely physical he yearns to spend time wallowing in basic animal activities—eating, sleeping, shitting, relaxing, and being soothed by Mama. Passive, rattle-headed Daddy's Girl, ever eager for approval, for a pat on the head, for the "respect" of any passing piece of garbage, is easily reduced to Mama, mindless minstrator to physical needs, soother of the weary, apey brow, booster of the puny ego, appreciator of the contemptible, a hot water bottle with tits.

VIVIAN: In front of the mirror I can make myself look like the most beautiful woman in the world, or with just a little change of makeup, the worst hag on the block. And it's all sight, eyes, seeing. Everything that matters is visual.

All the radiant beauty, all the ugly disasters. That's what television is all about. That's why it's going to change the world. It's not what the people on TV are saying that counts—what people are saying never really matters. It's what they look like they're doing . . . and how they look when they're doing it. That's the only form of communication that really matters . . . And most people don't do it very well at all . . .

GOLEM: We must wake people up. Upset their way of identifying things. It is necessary to create unacceptable images. Make people foam at the mouth. Force them to understand that they live in a mad world. A disquieting world, not reassuring. A world which is not as they see it.

BERNARD: Art is the market, nowadays; it can be defined only in those terms. Understand the marketplace and you understand the value of art. Buying and selling art today is like being a stockbroker; it has nothing to do with beauty, technique, originality, or catharsis of the soul.

From this point on, the great artists will come from the advertising industry. Of course, this may be disappointing to a few inspired youths who hold a paintbrush with a trembling hand, buy a piece of canvas with money scraped together by selling their shoes and family heirlooms . . . but hey—art is no longer for the weak of spirit. And if your spirit is weak, the advertising industry needs you.

DOROTHY *speaks to the audience.*

DOROTHY: I'm certainly not proud of what she did. When I go to the beauty parlor on Saturdays, all I hear is the snickering of women under hair dryers. Telling each other, pointing fingers. "Look, if it isn't Dorothy . . . You know about her daughter? . . . Shot Andy Warhol. A-N-D-Y W-A-R-H-O-L, that fairy New York artist that painted soup cans and made those god-awful disgusting pornographic films of homosexuals and naked heiresses. You know the fellow. Dorothy's daughter shot him. With a gun. Bam! Bam! Bam! Who could imagine?"

GOLEM: Am I anything more than the fear that others have of me? Is this important?

VIVIAN *leaves the dance stage and takes* VALERIE *by the hand, leading her to sit by the stump sculpture, downstage left.* VALERIE *calms down, they act like two best friends.*

LIGHTS: *Dim all stage except bring up glowing red and gold light around stump—like a campfire.*

MUSIC: *Lower volume or play something sweet and innocent.*

VIVIAN: I missed you! How was the hospital?

VALERIE: They tried to destroy me.

VIVIAN: Shock treatment?

VALERIE: Everything. They raped me twice.

VIVIAN: Oooh—did you report it to anyone?

VALERIE: If they think you're crazy no one listens.

VIVIAN: Why don't you tell me about it . . . I'll listen . . .

VALERIE: Okay, to men sexual relations is a redundancy. To call a man an animal is to flatter him; he's a machine, a walking dildo.

VALERIE *grows increasingly agitated.* VIVIAN *grows increasingly bored.*

VALERIE: It's often said that men use women. Use them for what? Surely not pleasure. It's females that are reduced to animals.

VIVIAN *stands and returns to little stage to dance again with* GOLEM. VALERIE *stands and begins pacing again, growing increasingly more agitated at the realization that no one will listen to her.*

VALERIE: Reducing the female to an animal, to Mama, to a male, is necessary for psychological as well as practical reasons: the male is a mere member of the species, interchangeable with every other male. He has no deep-seated individuality. Completely self-absorbed, males differ from each other only to the degree and in the ways they attempt to defend against their passivity and against their desire to be female.

DOROTHY: Every week I hear my friends laugh behind my back and I pretend not to. I don't say a word. Let them fill in the blanks on what happened to my Valerie. They don't deserve honesty. They're good people. Bridge and bowling, potlucks and family reunions. They can have it all. I've got Valerie, and no one can take her away.

DOROTHY *reaches out and grabs* VALERIE*'s hand.* VALERIE *reacts as if she's been bitten by a snake. All conversation ceases, and the stage goes into a hallucinogenic dark trip with slow strobe light flashing colored lights.*

All five actors begin to move in extreme slow motion.

Pre-informed AUDIENCE MEMBERS *are invited to come up on the stage to do various acts including, but not limited to, play music, adopt a pose of alienation, paint on a canvas, stare into a light, or make one or two striking remarks to themselves. At least one takes flash photos of the audience.*

SOUND *cue: Music is now a collage of Velvet Underground's "European Son" and opera or "Over the Rainbow" with occasional sound bites from TV commercials of 1968.*

During this slow-motion interlude, DOROTHY *is unable to concentrate on any one scene; she looks with fear and interest at the extras, at* BERNARD*, and most of all at* VALERIE*, who paces and speaks silently, without concern for audience.* GOLEM *and* VIVIAN *dance in extreme slow motion.*

When VALERIE *has had enough (approx. 3–4 minutes) she begins to orate, with her back to the audience. Once she starts to speak, lights come up and stage is cleared.*

VALERIE: The male is completely egocentric. Women don't have penis envy; men have pussy envy. The male is obsessed with screwing; he'll swim a river of snot, wade nostril-deep through a mile of vomit if he thinks there's a friendly pussy awaiting him. Screwing is a desperate, compulsive attempt to prove he's not passive, not a woman, but he is passive and does want to be a woman.

When the male accepts his passivity, and defines himself as a woman, he becomes a transvestite, loses his desire to screw, and gets his cock chopped off.

BERNARD *turns to speak to* DOROTHY, *who does not listen, but rather talks to him at the same time.*

BERNARD: Oh, I forgot to mention, about Beuys. Anyway, when Beuys left the gallery, for him the piece was over. But the gallery still had a cute little coyote urinating on its floors and whining for food, howling at the moon, and so forth.

The owner—a good friend of mine—didn't know quite what to do.

He considered releasing the coyote back into the wilderness, but it had become so domesticated through Beuys's piece, that to do so would be homicidal. He thought about donating it to the zoo, but Beuys's people were strictly opposed because it would be too demeaning to the coyote.

He finally just decided to keep it as a kind of pet, and prepared to bring it to his home.

But once outside the gallery door, the coyote was shocked by the noise and calamity of the street, and escaped. The rest of the story is tragic.

Apparently, a child tried to pet it, the coyote bit, the child lost a finger, the coyote was shot and killed by a rookie policeman.

I called Beuys with the sad news. He told me he felt as if his own brother had died.

I sent him a bottle of twenty-five-year-old Glen Farclas to cheer him up. Something about the morose effects of an exquisite single-malt scotch that makes any death in the family more enjoyable—er, bearable.

BERNARD *sips from a flask of scotch.*

DOROTHY: When Valerie decided to move to New York, she had already been living out of the house for a couple of years. We didn't get along very well in those days. She was staying in Baltimore, I had no idea where.

I wouldn't hear from her for months, then all of a sudden, she would call up and ask me to send her some money. I was not a rich woman, but I tried to send what I could. I mean, after all, she was my daughter and I did love her.

Then one day, she called and said she needed a little more money than usual because she was moving to New York to become a successful writer. I told her, "Valerie, honey, New York is a much bigger city than Baltimore. It's very rough there. People don't always succeed. I don't want you to get hurt." She just let me keep talking. There was nothing I could do. I thought I would never hear from her again. Then she called me from jail, and invited me here tonight.

VIVIAN *and* GOLEM *begin an erotic dance that leads to a near-sexual encounter.* GOLEM *slowly strips to bare naked.* VIVIAN *to her bra and stockings and boots.*

VIVIAN: Ooooh . . . that feels so good . . .

GOLEM: As smooth as oil . . .

VIVIAN: That's nice . . .

GOLEM: You're soo oo o nice . . .

VALERIE *watches, with increasing disgust.*

VALERIE: What's all this talk about nice? Nice? Nice! Mindless dribble. The more mindless the woman, the more deeply embedded she is in the male culture, in short, the "nicer" she is, the more sexual she is.

The nicest women in our society are raving sex maniacs. But, being just awfully, awfully nice, they don't, of course, descend to fucking—that's uncouth—rather they make love, commune by means of their bodies and establish sensual rapport. The literary ones are attuned to the throb of Eros and attain a clutch upon the Universe; the religious have spiritual communion with the Divine Sensualism; the mystics merge with the Erotic Principle and blend with the Cosmos, and acidheads contact all their erotic cells.

VIVIAN *and* GOLEM *are really into it now.*

VIVIAN: When you make love to me, I feel every cell I have start to spin into divinity.

BERNARD *discusses art with a statue, upstage, sipping from his flask occasionally.* DOROTHY *gets increasingly concerned about* VALERIE, *and files her nails to distract herself.*

VALERIE: Unhampered by propriety, niceness, discretion, public opinion, "morals," the "respect" of assholes, always funky, dirty, low-down, S.C.U.M. gets around. . . and around and around . . . they've seen the whole show—every bit of it—the fucking scene, the sucking scene, the dick scene, the dyke scene.

They've covered the whole waterfront, been under every dock and pier, the peter pier, the pussy pier . . . you've got to go through a lot of sex to get to anti-sex, and S.C.U.M.'s been through it all, and they're now ready for a new show: they want to crawl out from under the dock, move, take off, sink out.

But S.C.U.M. doesn't yet prevail; S.C.U.M.'s still in the gutter of our "society," which, if it's not deflected from its present course and if the Bomb doesn't drop on it, will hump itself to death.

DOROTHY: Valerie, honey, would you like to go home now?

VALERIE: I have no home!! *Pause.* Not yet. Not until all women simply leave men, refuse to have anything to do with any of them—ever. All men, the government, and the national economy would collapse completely.

DOROTHY: I've kept your room just the way it was when you left. I thought you'd like it that way.

VALERIE: In a sane society, the male would trot along obediently after the female. The male is docile, and easily led, easily subjected to the domination of any female who cares to dominate him. The male, in fact wants desperately to be led by females, wants Mama in charge, wants to abandon himself to her care. But this is not a sane society, and most women are not even dimly aware of where they're at in relation to men.

GOLEM *and* VIVIAN *continue to get down on each other.*

VIVIAN: I need you. You turn me into an animal.

GOLEM: We have entered into a centuries-old tradition.

DOROTHY: *(To* VALERIE.*)* Your father says hello.

VALERIE *hears the last comment from her mother and stares in disbelief, then becomes frenzied.*

VALERIE: Daddy only wants what's best for Daddy . . . peace and quiet, the opportunity to control and manipulate any sexual relations with his daughter.

A few examples of the most obnoxious or harmful types of men are: rapists, politicians, and all who are in their service; lousy singers and musicians; Chairmen of Boards; bread-winners; landlords; owners of greasy spoons and restaurants that play Musak; "Great Artists"; cheap pikers; cops; tycoons; scientists working on death and destruction programs or for private industry; liars and phonies; disc jockeys; men who intrude themselves in the slightest way on any strange female; real estate men; stock brokers; men who speak when they have nothing to say; men who loiter idly on the street and mar the landscape with their presence; double dealers; flim-flam artists; litterbugs; plagiarizers; men who in the slightest way harm any female; all men in the advertising industry; dishonest writers, journalists, editors, publishers; censors on both the public and private level; and all members of the armed forces.

DOROTHY: Honey, if you're hungry, there's salami—it's free!

GOLEM: *(To* VIVIAN.*)* We're making history.

VIVIAN: Make me like death, like heroin.

DOROTHY: Oh, and by the way Valerie, been meaning to ask you. Do you still see that sailor you used to date?

At this point VALERIE *goes hysterical and flaps her arms wildly during her next speech, eyeing each person at the party with increasing suspicion. While she rants,* BERNARD *addresses the audience.*

BERNARD: *(To* AUDIENCE.*)* You're curious about why I'm here. What is a respectable well-to-do man doing hanging around this crowd: Pill-popping crazed fags, drop-out heiresses, speed-freak cross-dressers, midgets, whores, artists (a few), all craving the attention and recognition of one man—Andy Warhol. I ask myself the same question every day. And the only answer I have is that in my life, being a part of this scene is the closest I'll ever get to being in love.

When every day, you wake up with fresh, vibrant expectations and a sense of—well, it's a funny word to use in this context . . . but in the faces of all these crazy people I see hope; even in the faces of those most full of despair.

And if that hope is ever completely removed from their face, they leave, or they are asked to leave. It's as simple as that. Laughter and tears, and a great artist behind all of it.

VALERIE: The conflict, therefore, is not between females and males, but between S.C.U.M.—dominant, secure, self-confident, nasty, violent, selfish, independent, proud, thrill-seeking, free-wheeling, arrogant females—and nice, passive, accepting, "cultivated," polite, dignified, subdued, dependent, scared, mindless, insecure, approval-seeking Daddy's Girls, who can't cope with the unknown, who want to continue to wallow in the sewer that is, at least, familiar, who want to hang back with the apes, who feel secure only with Big Daddy standing by, with a fat, hairy face in the White House, who can have a place in the sun, or rather, in the slime, only as soothers, ego boosters, relaxers, and breeders, who see the female as a worm.

VALERIE *suddenly swings a straight razor around. Threatens* BERNARD, *who drops to his knees.* VIVIAN *and* GOLEM *continue to writhe.* DOROTHY *is petrified, then mesmerized.*

BERNARD: Please, not me, Valerie! You can't—I'm innocent! I didn't do anything to you! Please just leave!

VIVIAN: Oh, yes, yes . . .

DOROTHY: This is just like the movies!

GOLEM: *(To* VIVIAN.*)* I like the way you cover your face.

GOLEM *and* VIVIAN *finish up rolling with a gasp and a shudder as* VALERIE *swings her straight razor in manic martial arts motions and approaches* GOLEM *(who, naked, suddenly notices the danger he's in).*

GOLEM: What are you doing?

VIVIAN *finally notices* VALERIE *and quickly starts putting her clothes back on, as frightened as the drugs will allow her to be.*

VIVIAN: Oh my God, Valerie. Stop. This isn't me, you're seeing . . . I was in a trance . . . a movie!

DOROTHY: Honey, put the knife down.

GOLEM: Go home, Valerie. Go back to jail. Get out—we don't want you here anymore.

VALERIE: I will not listen to you until you get on your knees and repeat to me one hundred times, "I am a turd, a lowly, abject turd," and then list all the ways in which you are.

DOROTHY: Everything's perfect the way it is. Nothing needs to be improved.

VALERIE: Women are improvable. Men are not. It lies in a woman's nature to look upon everything only as a means for conquering men. Dropping out is not the answer—fucking up is!

GOLEM: Put the knife away, Valerie.

VALERIE *grabs* GOLEM *(who is on his knees) and holds the knife to his throat.*

VIVIAN: Call the cops! I'm outta here.

VIVIAN *exits.*

GOLEM: No! No! Valerie, don't do it!

VALERIE: Don't struggle or kick or raise a fuss.

DOROTHY: Valerie, get away from him!

VALERIE: . . . Just sit back, relax, enjoy the show, and ride the waves to your demise.

GOLEM: NO!

With sudden adrenaline strength, DOROTHY *rips* VALERIE *off* GOLEM, *grips her around the neck, and begins to strangle her own daughter.*

DOROTHY: Why are you trying to hurt me like this? Haven't you hurt me enough? How can you do this to me? You still don't care about anyone but yourself!

BERNARD *and* GOLEM *watch in fascination.* VALERIE *struggles hard, finally breaks free, gasping, wheeling around, barely able to see. Focusing at last, she sees her mother.* DOROTHY *is livid and ready to kill.* VALERIE *becomes demure.*

VALERIE: Mama . . . I . . . love . . . you . . .

GOLEM *slaps* BERNARD *over the shoulder and guides him to the exit, while speaking.*

GOLEM: Hollywood is finally ready for us. I mean, *Midnight Cowboy?* No one in Hollywood would have touched it before *Chelsea Girls* became such a success. I just can't believe the irony—Andy Warhol's talking on the phone to Viva, when she's getting her hair dyed for big-budget Hollywood production *Midnight* motherfuckin' *Cowboy,* and he gets shot by Valerie Solanas and almost dies. . . . And now, Valerie wants him to get her on *Johnny Carson?*

We're all in the movies now. Every single situation of everyday life is now documented in some movie. All we have to do is remember which movie we liked best, and then—learn the role and say the words. Unless the movies invent new roles we'll all be bored soon. No wonder Andy didn't show up tonight.

VALERIE *is now in a post-shock therapy kind of babble-on. She quietly spews her diatribe, without feeling or passion, and wanders off the stage, back through the audience and out of the theater.*

VALERIE: The male "artist" . . . contempt for themselves . . . if they're good, that is, if they're nice . . . fraternizing with and trying to live through and fuse. . . . sexual feeling from "being a woman" . . . "culture" in short, "morals," the "respect" . . . our educational goal will be for a while to continue to think . . . secretly destroy . . . give things away . . . expose their vices . . . men who tell it like it is . . .

During VALERIE's *babble,* DOROTHY *finds her walker, slowly gets into position on it.*

SOUND *cue: Fade up final* MUSIC, *"Waiting for My Man."*

LIGHT *cue: Begin slow fade of lights as* DOROTHY *crosses stage to exit.*

DOROTHY: She had . . . a terrific sense of humor.

LIGHTS *fade to black except powerful* BLACK LIGHT, *which at full strength reveals previously hidden fluorescent additions to prints of Warhol's Marilyn Monroe faces on back wall. After few seconds of full strength, fade* LIGHTS.

BLACKOUT.

THE END

A TECHNO-K.O. IN 10 ROUNDS

ART WAS HERE

ART REVEALS ALL!

The underground club scene in London has tested it for 3 years. And now Virtual Resurrection is ready to come home. "I've always taken risks," says DJ Geno. For the first time on the West Coast, he plans to "resurrect" two legends from the past into today's hot ambient-techno club world: poet-boxer Arthur Cravan, the rebel whose wild antics sparked Dada, along with neo-fem-futurist Mina Loy.

"A KNOCKOUT PERFORMANCE! I THOROUGHLY DUG THE PLAY!!!"
LAURIE WIEGLER
SF WEEKLY

WRITER DIRECTOR **KATHI GEORGES** WITH **PETER CARLAFTES**
JEFF JOHNSON / BETH LISICK / JILLIAN MOSLEY

MARILYN MONROE MEMORIAL THEATER
96 LAFAYETTE / 11TH - 12TH - HOWARD / 552-3034 / FRI-SAT / 9PM / $10

ART WAS HERE

A Technical Knock Out in Ten Rounds
Featuring Poet–Pugilist Arthur Cravan

*Dedicated to
all who believe in
the power of creation.*

PRODUCTION NOTES:

Three Rooms Press's spiritual advisor is Arthur Cravan. No biography yet written has done him justice. In a world where everything is known through Wikipedia, Cravan remains an exception.

Arthur Cravan was a man who lived his life with the emphasis on choice. He was the nephew of Oscar Wilde. He was a boxer, winning the French National Boxing title without ever throwing a punch—he simply trash-talked his opponents so fiercely that each threw in the towel until no one was left, making Cravan the winner by default. He was a man who knew no bounds: his art was life and his canvas was the world.

Much of Cravan's life work influenced the Dada movement, from his magazine *Maintenant*, which he sold from a wheelbarrow outside a Paris racetrack, to his adamant anti-war stance, which led to his travels in North America during World War I and, ultimately, to his mysterious disappearance in a small boat off the coast of southwest Mexico in 1918.

I discovered Cravan through reading the excellent *The Lost Lunar Baedeker: Poems of Mina Loy*, edited and with an extensive introduction by Loy aficionado Roger Conover. I was fascinated, as Loy was, by this giant of a man. Near the end of her life, Loy was asked what had been the happiest times in her life. She replied: "Every moment spent with Arthur Cravan." And the unhappiest? "The rest of the time."

But how could I possibly expose the enormous energy of Cravan to a modern theater audience? I opted for juxtaposition. I had Cravan and Loy come "back to life" as three-dimensional projections at a modern-day rave festival, where crowds of partiers high on Ecstasy dance to repetitive beats feeling as "free" as the promoter encourages them to believe`. Cravan, never one to buy in to any propaganda, quickly sees through the money-grubbing fame games of the promoter and wreaks havoc of the most delicious kind.

—*K. G.*

ART WAS HERE
A Technical Knock Out in Ten Rounds
Featuring Poet–Pugilist Arthur Cravan

CHARACTERS:

ARTHUR CRAVAN:
Poet–pugilist–projection; "I am the focal point of the world"

MINA LOY:
Poet–artist–projection; "I am the center of a circle of pain"

GENO:
Promoter, deejay; "'S'up?"

REF:
Protégé; "You both know the rules."

SETTING:

One night at Club Geno, an underground rave club run by the beloved world famous deejay GENO, *who promises an eclectic atmosphere of freedom. Admission by invitation only. The Deejay Booth overlooks an (unseen) main dance floor and is accessible only by staff/security badge. Room has two turntables, and full deejay setup. Near deejay equipment is a table with Geno's special punch and a few cups. The Retrofied Forest is a "chill" room with a quieter vibe and green lighting designed to make it look like an indoor forest. Seating in this room is park benches. The Control Room is a backstage area with monitors, first aid, folding chairs, and supplies. The Main Stage is an area that is generally unseen, and would feature go-go dancers, until used in Round Nine and Ten of this play.*

ROUND ONE
Deejay Booth

As the audience enters the theater, GENO *deejays, dancing behind his turntables, carefully selecting each new record. A pitcher of punch sits on a table nearby. The stage is dim blue. The house area is lit by blinking* LIGHTS. *As* LIGHTS *fade, an intense slow song begins. The house* LIGHTS *blink slower and slower until they are out.*

GENO *crosses to* USR. *Fills glass of punch.* ART *enters* DSL, *crossing slowly, as if pulled by the vibration. Hunched over like an old man. Punching air weakly.* GENO *sees* ART *in mirror. They stare at each other's reflections.*

GENO: *(To mirror.)* You looking for something? It ain't here.

Waits for response. Gets none. ART *punches his own reflection.*

GENO: Hey—The head's down the hall. This is Backstage. You got a pass?

ART *punches* GENO's *reflection.*

GENO: *Still looking in mirror, fixing hair.* Hey—You got an all-access pass? Put it on. You don't got one? Get out. *Takes punch back to turntables.* You listening?

ART *punches his own reflection. Crosses to punch. Pours a cup. Sniffs it. Pours it back. Sees* GENO's *records. Pulls one out, takes off the sleeve. Examines record.*

GENO: *Angry.* Hey—Put that back—That's my shit! What you doing? You in the wrong club, or something. We don't take requests here. I'm in control of this mix. *Picks up sleeve.* Hey—*Laughs.* Heeeeyyyy . . . At least you got good taste. What d'ya know? My fav-o-rite tune. It's so rare . . . hypnotic . . . very eclectic. I call this here tune . . . "The Dream Disconnected" . . . Yeah . . . German import. Hard to find . . . It's collectible . . . Now go on downstairs and I'll mix it in for you . . .

ART *lifts needle on record that's playing.*

GENO: 'S'up? Oh, man! Shit! What the— . . . *Tries to push* ART *away from turntable.* ART *puts his fists up.* GENO *backs off.*

Hey, man! No one fucks with my records! Shit! That's it, man! I'm calling . . . security, man! *Into headphones.* Hey! Security! Security! We got a problem! Control Room!

(To ART.*)* Security's coming.

ART *starts warming up to fight.*

GENO: Hey—'S'up wid you, man! Security's coming! Get out while you can. If Security finds you, you're dead.

Fade up SOUND *of crowd at a boxing match.* LIGHTS *change to define a boxing ring on stage.*

ART *picks up tempo.*

GENO: *Downs punch.* Security! Control Room! Security! Hey!'S'up!

VOICEOVER: In the blue corner, wearing gold, 170 pounds, defending the light heavyweight champion of paradise, Ladies and Gentlemen, The Dream Disconnector . . . The Man in the Booth! . . . Geno! *Crowd cheers.*

GENO: Hey—What's going on? What's happenin'! That's me!

Enter REF.

51

GENO: 'S'up? 'S'up? Tell me—'S'up? *Downs more punch.*

VOICEOVER: *Cutting off* GENO. And in the red corner, wearing red, weighing 174—

ART: *Cuts off* VOICEOVER. I do my own intro. I'm a swindler, a pirate, a poet, and a whore. No one can stop me. I need to be stopped. No one can stop me. I need to be stopped. *(Repeat.)*

GENO: *During* ART*'s speech, fearful.* You hear what he's saying? Stop him! Stop him! You gotta do something!

REF: *Blows whistle. Two short blasts. Moves to center ring.* Okay . . .You both know the rules . . . Let's have . . . a clean fight. I mean . . . No low hits . . . no trouble . . . A knockdown means the man on his feet retreats until I give him the signal . . . Good luck, Geno. Good luck, Art.

GENO: You're Art!

REF: Fight fair!

ART: I'm Art!

REF: Let's go!

GENO: But—

ART: I'm Art . . .

GENO: —you look—

ART: I'm Art.

GENO: —normal. They said—

REF: Let's go!

GENO: —you were—

ART: I'm Art.

GENO: —hip—they said—

ART: I'm Art.

REF: Time's up—

GENO: —you were—

ART: I'm Art—

ART: Let's go—

GENO: —cool—

REF: —ready?—

GENO: I can't—

ART: Stop me. . .

GENO: —believe it—

REF: Start fighting!

GENO: What?

ART: I'm history. You're dust.

GENO: Don't let him hurt me!

REF: It's all up to you.

MINA: *From* OFFSTAGE. Stop the fight! Stop the fight! *Throw in white scarf.*

SOUND: *Bell rings.* BLACKOUT.

END OF ROUND ONE

ROUND TWO
The Retrofied Forest

MINA: Arthur . . . Arthur . . . Arthur . . . Where are you? . . . Arthur?

LIGHTS *up.* SOUND *of birds chirping at dawn.*

MINA: *Wandering, as if through a forest.* Arthur? . . . Arthur? . . . *Sinks on bench.* Arthur. He left. He died. Who knows what happens? I spent years looking . . . I had to give up . . . the way widows do . . . you need to go on. . . . Sometimes . . . I see . . . an image of him . . . so detailed, so clear . . . I reach out . . . I feel heat . . . his cheek . . . I reach. . . . Something stops me from touching . . . a memory . . . a look . . . He never liked to be touched. . . . He knew hands . . . absolutely. . . . The way that they murder . . . caresses disguised with murmurs of love . . . how quickly . . . they slide down the throat of the victim . . . how quickly . . . the suffocation begins . . .

ART *enters. Wanders through trees begins listening. Looks at his hands. Sneaks up behind* MINA. *Begins strangling her playfully.*

ART: Guess who?

MINA: *Caught up in dejection. Defends herself instinctively, without heart.* Help.

ART: *Climbing over bench to sit beside her.* It's me!

MINA: Arthur.

ART: Arthur's too . . . retro. Call me Art.

MINA: I'm hallucinating . . .

ART: Don't worry. . . . You look great. What brought you here?

MINA: I was invited. Fabi's granddaughter Amber . . . *Suddenly proud.* Your great granddaughter . . . . plays didgeridoo in a techno-trance band. . . .

ART: Oh, Jesus! What's that?

MINA: It's new! It's important! It's what the kids want!

ART: Don't tell me it's what that deejay was playing.

MINA: Geno's her boyfriend. This is his club.

ART: That asshole gets all the dough?

MINA: Yes. He's innovative. He's rich. He's sort of a legend.

ART: Who wants to be a legend?

MINA: You did.

Pause.

ART: Remember when you and I met? Long ago. We spent whole nights together on benches like this. Central Park—in the spring . . . talking till dawn. You read your poetry. . . .

MINA: You told stories. You were—

ART: You were red hot!

MINA: —the only intelligence I could converse with.

Pause.

ART: What's that poem of yours . . . about pain?

MINA: Which one?

ART: You know—the one you wrote before we met? "I am the center of . . ."

MINA: . . . a circle of pain . . . *Continues.*

ART: That's the one. How's it go?

MINA: . . . exceeding its boundaries in every direction. . . . The business of the bland sun has no affair with me in my congested cosmos of agony. . . . Pain is no stronger than the resisting force pain calls up in me. The struggle is equal. . . . A moment being realization can— vitalized by cosmic initiation—furnish an adequate apology for the objective agglomeration of activities of a life . . . LIFE . . . a leap with nature into the essence . . . the was-is-ever-shall-be of cosmic reproductivity. Rises from the subconscious impression of a cat with blind kittens among her legs . . . same undulating life-stir . . . I am that cat. That same undulation of living . . . death . . . life . . . I am knowing . . . all about . . . unfolding. . . .

During poem, ART *remains enraptured. Secretly draws with chalk on the bench "Art was Here."*

As MINA *recites poem,* GENO *enters and begins sneaking around behind them. Taking notes. As she finishes, he is focusing camera. The whole time he talks to himself.*

GENO: I can't believe—that agent's crazy! I ain't paying a dime! To him or the techies! The catalog showed a hip freak! What do I get? A regular human being. I ain't paying for this! I'll get proof—I'll sue them for every cent that they got! Hey, you two—SMILE!

ART: No pictures! *Rises—advances to beat him up.*

GENO: Look—I'm trying to focus! Sit down and shut up.

ART: *(To* MINA.*)* This guy says shut up? *(To* GENO.*)* Hey—is that what you said?

GENO: Security. To the Retrofied Forest. *(To* ART.*)* Don't get so excited—it's bad for your heart.

ART: My heart? *(To* MINA.*)* This guy's looking out for my heart. *(To* GENO.*)* I love this guy! Hey—You're beautiful, man! You think my heart's bad—what about yours? You better hope it's still ticking when I get through with you—

GENO: Security! Hurry! Get away from me or you're dead!

ART: Ha! Did you forget? We're already dead!

MINA: Dead? Are we dead?

GENO: Dead or alive, no fighting's allowed. War is extinct. Conquered by love.

ART: *Advances fists up.* Let's go, pal! Let's talk about love!

Enter REF. GENO *points at* ART.

REF: Him again. . . . Okay . . . you both know the rules.

GENO: I told him one of the rules is we don't allow fighting.

REF: How can you fight if no fighting's allowed?

ART: By knowing Rule 1. All rules are invalid. *Pulls out rule book, hands it to* REF. See for yourself. Here's the rulebook.

MINA: I don't feel dead. Do I look dead? *Pulls mirror out of her purse. Looks at it. Corrects her makeup.*

REF: *Thumbing through rulebook.* Hmmm. . . . Let's see. Rule 1.

ART: *(To* MINA.*)* You're beautiful!

MINA: But I'm dead.

GENO: *Back to camera.* I got to stay focused . . .

REF: *Steps between* GENO/*camera and* ART/MINA. Here it is: Rule 1: All rules are invalid. He's right, Geno!

ART *grabs book back. Sneaks off stage.*

GENO: Shut up! *Pushing* REF *out of way.* Okay, Say cheese! Hey! What happened? Where'd he go?

MINA: *Turns to look. Reads "Art Was Here." Runs* OFFSTAGE *after him.* Arthur! Art! Wait for me!

GENO: *(To* REF.*)* Hurry up! Get them! Don't let them mingle!

Exit REF.

SOUND: *Bell rings.* LIGHTS *fade on* GENO *angrily erasing* ART's *sign.*

END OF ROUND TWO

ROUND THREE
Control Room

LIGHTS *up.* ART *and* MINA *enter.*

ART: We'll be safer here. You can't hide in a crowd.

Offstage GENO *and* REF *are heard arguing.* ART *and* MINA *hide under turntable stand.*

REF: They disappeared.

GENO: Shit! You didn't find him?

REF: I looked everywhere.

Enter GENO *and* REF.

GENO: Why didn't you stop him?

REF: He didn't break any rules.

GENO: Give me that rulebook.

REF: He took it back.

GENO: You mean it was his? You fuckin' idiot! I'm the one paying you! You don't use his rulebook! *Grabs* REF. In here, we go by my rules!

REF: What rules? Where's your rulebook?

GENO: I don't need one. You know why?

REF: No. *Sits at punch table, rolling cigarettes.*

GENO: I'll tell you. It's in the punch. My rulebook! It's all in this punch. My special punch. They drink it all night. . . . 'Cause they know the punch makes them feel good. That's all they want. Look at their faces. All smiles. All love. They dance. They watch. They follow the rules . . . thinking, like you, that there are none.

REF: "Do whatever you want." That's your motto, right?

GENO: Isn't it great? What a concept! A little punch and—boom!—you're set free. You don't really do anything—but at least you know no one will stop you.

REF: I could stop them. But you won't let me interfere. Why am I here?

GENO: Without your uniform it wouldn't be fun. Take a thief. Does a thief rob a bank just for money? No! The real thrill, the whole kick, is getting away with it. If we just told everyone here "Do whatever you want?"—would they enjoy themselves? No! They'd be bored. They need a guard, a watchdog, an institution to conquer. They see you—a uniform—they don't get hassled—that's it!—they think they controlled you. Love power! Tell your friends. Bring 'em next week. Pack the place. Pretty soon, it's a movement. A rebellion. The next revolution. Thanks to you—

REF: I get it, I get it. So how come tonight—all of a sudden—you screaming at me to keep people in line?

GENO: Tonight's different. This Art? He's not drinking the punch. He doesn't want to feel good. He's a crack in the illusion. As our maintenance specialist—you gotta stop him.

REF: Maintenance specialist? You mean—like a janitor? A garbage collector?

GENO: Stop whining—without me you'd still be working the streets.

REF: You think this is better?

GENO: Stay focused. We gotta problem at hand. I need you, tonight . . . to get rid of the trash.

REF: What—You want me—to kill them?

GENO: They're already dead.

REF: I didn't do it! It wasn't me!

GENO: I'm not blaming you. Calm down and listen. These guys aren't alive. They've been dead thirty years. They're Virtual Resurrections. First time on the West Coast. London clubs got the idea three years ago. It's old hat to them now—but here, it's just starting.

REF: I don't get it.

GENO: We're in on the ground floor of the next big thing! Virtual Resurrection! The concept's so simple! They developed a way to bring people back to life. Not really alive—they're just 3-D projections—but they look real, they sound real—what more do you want? They got 2,000 names so far . . . some really cool people—Jimi, Janis, Picasso, Elvis. I was all hot for Hendrix till I looked at the price tag—you wouldn't believe what they get for the stars. It's in the eight figure range—I was shocked, let me tell you. I can't take that risk. Not yet anyway. I ran through the whole list, and wouldn't you know. Only one name's in our price range. Art. I say, "Who the hell's Art?" They get me his agent. Shows me some clippings, says kids go nuts. Kept saying, "Wait till you see his punch," I think yeah—punch—sure, great! All I know is he's cheap. So I book him, no problem, you know—everything's cool. Then, last week, like, Amber checks out the flyer—she goes,

"Wow!"—I'm like, "What—did we spell your name wrong?"—
she's like, "No way!"—I'm like, "Calm down"—she's like, "Art!
Art!"—you know why?—turns out he's her long lost great
granddad. I think, Cool, I did something right for a change. But
is it enough? No! Not for Amber! She goes, she says, "You gotta
get Mina!" I go, "Who's Mina?" She goes, "Mina Loy." I go, "Myrna
Loy—what? the actress?" And she goes, "No, Mina—my great
grandmother—you know—the poet." I say, "Poet?—like on
MTV?" She goes yeah. I go, "Bay shrimp"—that's what I call
her—I say, "Bay shrimp, I can barely afford Art. Do you know
what it costs?" I start talking hard figures, and she gets all like
crying—she's just comin' down off the E, I figure—give her a
day. But the next day it's worse. The bitch won't let up! Says she's
callin' the cops to check out the punch. She screaming and
screaming. What could I do? I work out a deal to make Amber
happy. Great. And what do I get? A little less cash and a nightmare
in paradise.

REF: Less cash my ass! I've never seen it so packed!

GENO: That's the problem. If this mob listens to these two, they'll all
turn at once.

REF: No one will listen to them. They're too normal looking.

GENO: That's why they're dangerous. Their ideas are weird, not their
appearance. They aren't freaks. They don't look like performers.
Take the old man—no big hair, no fetishes, no scars, no tattoos—
he's perfectly normal. And the broad—hell, I tell you—she's
Amber in ten years. Same eyes, same nose—without all the
piercings. These two fit in—that's why they're dangerous. They
aren't about tricks. They're regular people. Anyone could do
what they do. If the crowd bites—Jesus!—we're history—we're
dust—the feel-good mirage will instantly shatter—by the end of
the night we'll both be looking for work.

REF: I could use a new job—where I get some respect. Even a garbage collector deserves some respect.

GENO: Respect? You think I don't respect you? We've been together—how long? Couple of years? Remember when we first started—in the back room on King Street—stapling flyers on street poles, calling friends, borrowing turntables? We struggled and why? It wasn't the money! It was the dream! From the very beginning you were always there—on time. You were dependable. You never once let me down. I could count on you. I got nothing but respect for you, baby. You're not an employee. You're a real honest-to-god Friend. *Sniffles.* Okay—I was gonna surprise you. But I can't keep it secret. Why not tell you right now? I've got plans for you. Big plans. A VIP room. You run it—we split the bar down the middle. You'll have total control. A room of your own. We'll start—next Tuesday—it's a real opportunity. What do you think?

REF: You're lying.

GENO: Friends don't lie to each other.

REF: You're not bullshitting me?

GENO: Do you think I would do that? After all we've been through?

REF: I'll be in charge? I can do what I want?

GENO: For as long as you want to.

REF: When I was a kid, I used to dream about having my own room. I always had to share—with my sisters—you know?—we had a big family—I was the middle kid. I didn't have a choice. And then—later?—there were roommates or lovers—I don't know—someone telling me what to do . . .

GENO: Kid—you help me with my dream, I'll help you with yours. Security. The punch. Are you in?

REF: I'm floored. VOICEOVER *counts like a knockout. On five,* REF *gets up.* A room of my own? I could smoke there and everything. I'll clean the whole house for that. *Exits. Smacking fist into hand.*

GENO: *Laughs.* Oh—hey! Check the Forest. People always try to go back where they came from.

SOUND: *Bell rings.*

ART *peeks out from under table as* GENO *exits.* Fade LIGHTS.

END OF ROUND THREE

ROUND FOUR
Control Room

ART *helps* MINA *get out from under table.*

MINA: Finally. *Sneezes.* I thought he'd never stop talking.

ART: What does Amber see in him?

MINA: Money.

ART: A gold digger—I knew it. Beats working for a living.

MINA: She likes to be comfortable. Why be a starving artist if you don't have to? Nothing's wrong with having a warm bed to sleep in.

ART: Comfort tempts people to disappear. Warm beds are another story. Remember? Let's go get a room—like we did in the old days?

MINA: There's not enough time. You gotta be on stage in twenty minutes.

ART: Let them wait. Better yet cancel the show.

MINA: We can't. It's the only reason we're here.

ART: Who cares why we're here? All I know is I'm going crazy for you.

MINA: I'm hot for you too. But . . .

ART: Let's go!

MINA: No . . . it's not safe.

ART: The world hasn't changed.

MINA: It's the fear . . . I remember . . .

ART: Stop worrying!

MINA: What about money? I don't have a dime.

ART: These kids are loaded. I'll pick a few pockets.

MINA: But these are nice people. They came to see you.

ART: You're right. They're so nice they're dying to help us. Why pick their pockets? We'll just mention we're horny and broke and like magic, they'll suggest a hotel, hand us two hundred bucks and say, "Have fun!" Nice people. You can tell just by looking!

MINA: Stop being so cynical.

ART: You don't approve? Don't worry. For you, baby—I'll be—the cutest little optimist you ever did see. *Smiles.* Is this smile okay, honey? I have to breathe now. Do you want me to use my right lung or my left?

MINA: *Cuts him off.* All right . . . you win. Let's get a room.

ART: No. You'd be frustrated. *Pretends to play a record.* Let's dance.

ART *dances with* MINA. SOUND *cue: Unrhythmic noises and beats.*

ART: Sounds great, doesn't it?

MINA: This music?

ART: No, silly! The beating of my heart.

MINA: Is that what we're listening to? Call the hospital.

ART: This is my song—the only song I can dance to.

MINA: It's . . . interesting.

ART: It goes on forever.

MINA: I'm already sweating.

ART: Here, take off your coat. . . . *Takes it off.* Look at you. . . . You're blushing.

MINA: Embarrassed—a leftover habit.

ART: You? Embarrassed? I can't believe it! The Mina I knew was one tough broad.

MINA: I . . . I came from a place where the weather changed quickly. . . . Even on hot days, I wore a coat . . . so the cold—if it came—wouldn't affect me. I did not want to appear to be cold. A sudden drop in temperature makes coatless people savage; desperate for warmth they shiver and curse, steal, kill. I laughed at these fools, exposed as the brute I would never be. I despised the heat, and worshipped cold and night. It set me apart. I thought I was brilliant. I thought my coat was me. One tough broad. But it wasn't. I never knew till you left how cold I could be.

ART: Brrr . . .

MINA: Do me a favor—hit me—right now. In the face, go ahead. I should be crying by now. And look—no tears! I want to feel something.

ART: You hit me first. Come on—hard as you can. There's no reason not to. We can't feel pain anymore. Or joy, or love. But the habit's still there. All the habits.

MINA: *Pinching herself.* It's not numb. It just doesn't hurt like before. *She hits* ART. *He smiles.* I never did that to anyone. I didn't think I could.

ART: Okay, your turn. *Hits* MINA. *She looks in the mirror.*

MINA: Not a scratch. Doesn't hurt. Do it again!

They hit each other in slow motion, each punch announced in slow motion speech, and responded to in exaggerated slow motion joy/tears/anger/ shock.

MINA: I feel so alive.

ART: Just think what you missed all those years that you were.

Punches her shoulder. They turn their backs to each other and touch hands lightly, then step away from each other.

During fight, REF *enters.*
End of song, REF *whistles loudly. Grabs* MINA *and tries to handcuff her.*

REF: Just come along quietly and there won't be trouble.

ART: Hands off!

REF: You can't hurt me. You're dead. You're not real. You're just a projection.

ART: But you're not! *Hits* REF. REF *grabs head with both hands.*

REF: Hey! That hurt!

MINA: *Laughing.* Did you like it?

REF: I hate pain.

MINA: *Laughs. Pats* REF's *shoulder.* You'll love it when you're dead.

REF: What's it like to be dead? I mean—you seem to be having a good time.

ART: You call this a good time? You should have seen me in the old days.

MINA: Yeah, even our emotions are just projections. We don't feel anything. Like you.

REF: Most of the time I don't feel very good. I put on an act. For the crowd. I don't want to be like the crowd.

ART: Then why do you stay here?

REF: I don't know. It's easier to remain where you are. I get respect from all sides. Geno just told me I get to run my own VIP room— starting next Tuesday.

ART: What does he get out of it?

REF: Half the bar. And—oh, yeah—he wants me to arrest you guys.

MINA: Why?

REF: He thinks you'll turn everyone against him.

ART: What do you think?

REF: I try not to.

ART: Tell you what—I like you—let's have some fun.

REF: *Warily.* Okay . . .

ART: Let's get Geno!

MINA: Yeah!

ART: Now—handcuff us—God! Look at these things! All show—
like everything else around here. Bring us to Geno. We'll take
care of the rest.

REF: Why should I trust you?

ART: Because I decided you should. Let's go—where is he?

REF: *Handcuffing them.* The Retrofied Forest.

ART: I knew it! He's so consistent.

SOUND: *Bell rings.* BLACKOUT.

END OF ROUND FOUR

ROUND FIVE
The Retrofied Forest

GENO *sits on bench in Retrofied Forest.*

GENO: Where are they? I got to stop them. *Enter* ART, *handcuffed to* MINA. GENO *sees* ART. *Shudders, then regains composure seeing* REF *following behind them.* It's about time. . . . Here sit down.

REF: I got them, boss! I got them!

GENO: Settle down! Security didn't hurt you, I hope. I know things have been a little rough tonight. But—let's try again, shall we? Welcome to my club! I'm Geno, and I just want to say—I'm so glad you're here. *(To* MINA.*)* Amber showed me your poetry . . . fabulous . . . you use words so . . . well . . . I'm so honored to make your acquaintance tonight. *(To* ART.*)* And you, my good man . . . *Little punch on the shoulder. Little man-to-man laugh.* You son-of-a gun . . . I know all about you . . . you're a legend . . . these kids are dying to see you. . . . This show's a sell-out . . . and you know why? . . . The flyer— "ART REVEALS ALL." What a thrill. The phone's been ringing off the hook!

ART: Believe me, the pleasure's all mine. *Winks at* MINA.

GENO: That's right! What a guy! You're beautiful, baby!

MINA: This place is huge.

ART: And so crowded. Why, I've never seen so many nice people before.

GENO: Well—lemme tell you. Couple years ago I had a vision of sorts—of a new world—where people could just be themselves for a change. The way I figure, the people are darn sick and tired of being told what to do, how to dress, how to talk, etc., etc. You know what I'm saying. No—they weren't stupid—they just needed an outlet. A place to begin, where their minds could be challenged without interference. Through music. Performances. Lectures. *(To* MINA.*)* Poetry. A place where the imagination was free to unfold. A place where reality wasn't a problem. Can I create such a place? I said, "I can." And now, after only two years, you can see the results. A cutting-edge cybersex hypnotic environment.

ART: Can it stop time?

GENO: *Mock serious.* Not yet . . . *Laughs.* But we're working on it. We open Friday at eight and don't shut down till midnight on Sunday. Half the crowd stays here all weekend . . . and yet? People complain the time just passed too quickly.

MINA: What do they do all that time?

GENO: They watch . . . or dance . . . or let their minds wander. It's not an escape, it's a new way of life.

ART: Yeah—I saw your infomercial. You got a hell of a copywriter— who'd you use? A pro firm, or a cheap, hot new talent? What's your take for this weekend—did you cover expenses? What'd they clip you for me? Were you able to grind them? This place is so clean—that must cost you a bundle. This new way of life is a fantastic idea! Must make you feel proud to be the guy in control. You got plans for expansion? Why bother closing? Once this thing catches on, they'll beg you to stay open. And once they start begging—you can make them do anything. They'll see you as a virtual fountain of hope. They'll trust you, depend upon you for the answers. And as long as they pay—you'll give them your answers. But you can't give them what they want more than anything else. You can't give them a way to stop time for themselves. And they'll grow old, Geno, they'll grow old for a cause. They'll die for a cause—your cause, not theirs—and it won't be enough—they'll die screaming for more. More time!

More time! I've heard it enough. But you can't give them that—you can only subtract it by directing their minds to a repeating beat. Like the beat you march to yourself—money, power—as though time is illusion—a trifling concern. You don't notice it slipping out of your hands. You don't notice your hands. You don't notice anything outside the beat because you're afraid it might hurt. And believe me—it hurts—to give up your masters. It hurts. Till you decide it doesn't hurt anymore. And you can't decide that if you're only a slave.

GENO: I've got tricks. New technology. There's no need to die now. Look at yourselves. You're living proof.

MINA: We're dead.

GENO: No one can tell you apart from the others. You fit right in.

ART: That's what scares me the most. That's why I'm here. Watch . . . *Rushes over to* MINA *and punches her stomach.*

GENO: Hey! Stop that!

MINA: Why? I don't feel a thing.

ART: *Caresses her cheek. No reaction.* She used to melt when I touched her. Now pleasure's just an idea. It can't be experienced, only described.

GENO: So what? You're dead. These people are living.

ART: They're living dead. And you are responsible.

Begins to attack. REF *rushes in.*

REF: Get him! Kill him!

GENO: Help me! *Falls flat on ground. Begin count.*

REF: Okay, guys, that's enough for now. Let's take him to the Control Room and get him cleaned up. *Picks* GENO *up by the heels. Drags him offstage.*

GENO: I respected you!

REF: You expect me to believe that?

SOUND: *Bell rings.* BLACKOUT.

END OF ROUND FIVE

ROUND SIX
Deejay Booth

In the office. REF *is putting bandages on* GENO *next to turntables.* ART *is on floor near punch table searching through bag.* MINA *is writing on back center wall. Muffled didgeridoo music is heard.*

REF: Okay, hold still . . .

GENO: Ouch! Be careful!

REF: Stop jerking your head all over the place.

GENO: I'm not moving!

REF: Almost finished. Don't flinch.

GENO: Cocksucker!

REF: You're one to talk! All done. Hmmm . . . I like it. *Turns* GENO *to mirror.* Whaddya think?

GENO: *Looking in mirror.* Aggh! *Looks away. Slowly looks back.* Painful. Absolutely painful.

REF: It's a good look for you. Rugged. Street-wise. But hey—it's your head. Live with it for a week—you don't like it, come back—

GENO: I'm ruined.

REF: —follow-ups are always free.

GENO: What will Amber say? *Looks in mirror.* I'm finished. *Looks closer, not at wounds but at first signs of wrinkles around his eyes.*

REF: Oh my God—you been listening to her set? Awful. Sounds like your face.

MINA: *Listens to music. overlaps* REF *and* GENO. Oh, I can't get over this music! It's just like . . . floating underground.

ART: Have you seen my mouthpiece?

MINA: *Unaware.* Listen to that music, Arthur. Can you believe that's your great-granddaughter? I've never heard anything like it.

ART: *No response. Continues looking for mouthpiece. Frustrated not finding it. Vocalizes every thought about this. Dumps out athletic bag. Puts each article back in one at a time.*

GENO: She hasn't slept for three days. I'm surprised she showed up.

REF: Everyone shows up for the paying gigs. . . . What I always wonder is . . . what do they do in-between? Take you and Amber, for instance. What do you do when you're not here? How do the two of you spend your evenings at home? Surely it's not one continuous party. I'll bet you do something fantastic. Tell me. I can't imagine . . .

GENO: We do . . . things . . . you know. . . evenings . . . like anyone else.

REF: For example—who cooks?

GENO: No one. We eat out.

REF: Who cleans?

GENO: The maid.

REF: A maid! Frees you up from the drudgery of household chores. Gives you an edge—all that extra time. . . . So—let's see—you don't cook, you don't clean—you're home—you and Amber—together—what do you do?

GENO: We relax.

REF: You relax! Ahh—the leisurely life. Watch TV, play cards, maybe read a good book. And later—it's bedtime—there's lots to do there. I bet she's a tiger with all her experience.

GENO: She's not bad.

MINA: Arthur—you hear Amber? Such . . . ethereal music.

ART: I know I brought it. Where the hell is it? *Dumps bag out again.*

MINA: She's on her last song now . . .

REF: Not bad? So why are you always out cruising the streets? That's where we met—remember—on the street? You knew Bryan already—my good buddy, Bryan—he was our common denominator—he introduced me to you as his friend—he said "friend"—and next thing you know, the three of us were very intimate. A full day of leisure. Then back home to Amber for an evening of relaxation. She must have been so happy to see you. She couldn't have known—you're a very discreet man. Very . . . discreet.

GENO: Can we focus on Problem At Hand . . . ?

REF: Oh yes . . . Trouble in Paradise. *Pulls flask out of pocket. Sips.* You want some of this?

GENO *takes flask. Drinks a sip. Chokes a little.*

REF: Easy, there, Geno. It's not punch, you know.

GENO *sips again without choking. Puts flask in pocket.*

REF: Give it back.

GENO *is confused, then surprised. Hands flask back grudgingly. Looks back into mirror.*

REF: Trouble in Paradise. Very many problems. Very few solutions.

GENO: Very funny. Shit—I can't go on stage like this.

REF: Sure you can—scarification is sexy . . .

GENO: Get away from me.

REF: You never said that before.

GENO: I didn't need to . . . we were on the same team. If this guy could make you switch sides so easily, just think what he'll do with this crowd—

REF: I don't play for nobody but myself. Not you, not him—

GENO: He's got you believing that crap? That's it—he's not going on stage.

REF: You signed a contract.

GENO: Let him sue me.

REF: The crowd won't buy it. I'll spread rumors. You can't hide.

GENO: Please—help me one last time! I need you . . . OUCH!

REF: Why suddenly all out of whack? Where's that old disconnection? If I didn't know better, I'd say you were falling apart, Geno.

MINA: *(To* ART.*)* Well, it's over. You missed it.

ART: I heard it. She's awful.

MINA: What? Amber?

ART: It stunk.

MINA: You shouldn't say that.

ART: I did . . .

GENO: *Speaking to* REF *while looking at mirror.* Do I look . . . different to you?

REF: Come here. Let's have a look-see. GENO *slowly turns and walks over with some difficulty.* Hmmm . . . REF *examines* GENO's *face—each eye, teeth, nose, ear, hair.* Hmmm . . . a few bruises . . . cuts . . . other than that . . . nothing unusual . . .

GENO: I feel old. You know, like, all of a sudden. I think my hair's turning gray. I'm getting wrinkles.

REF: It's that pout. Try smiling.

GENO *attempts a weak smile.*

REF: That's it. No pain. No pain.

GENO: No pain. No p— Ouch! My mouth. *Rushes back to the mirror.* I must have a chipped tooth or something.

REF: *Crosses to mirror. Rubs* GENO*'s back.* Poor baby. Poor, poor, little baby. What's the matter—a few punches wipe out the dream? Or did they jar loose a memory you thought you'd disposed of? You're setting a very bad example for the punch crowd. The show must go on! Get out there and fight. They're waiting for you. Isn't that why you're here?

MINA: What didn't you like?

ART: You already know. . . . Do I have to explain? Okay—let me tell you about Amber and her fellow musicians. . . . They played some songs with some unusual instruments—the notes were in tune; no one missed a beat. People will applaud. They'll get paid. Even though nothing happened. Every song. Horrible. There was no growth. . . . For forty-five minutes they wasted water . . . wasted it on plastic houseplants to convince us they were real. Their tricks fooled some people, as tricks always do. These same people then fool others. The mirage expands . . . joy contracts. Look around— under the smiles? So much sorrow, caused by a million incarnations of illusions that have nothing to do with the earth as it is . . .

REF *crosses to sit at* ART*'s feet, enraptured, like* MINA.

ART: . . . I could say I've been to another place where one night I heard a similar song . . . sitting on soil . . . under stars . . . I could say I cried in the soil . . . rolled in the soil . . . licked the soil . . . listened . . . to a song beyond the limits of language. I could say I remember this soil . . . but not before now . . .

GENO, *while* ART *is speaking, slowly sneaks away.*

REF: Did you hear that, Geno? Hey—he's gone. Aw—good riddance. Who needs him? *Lies down.*

ART: I do . . . I want to watch him hurt. *Exits.*

SOUND: *Bell rings.* BLACKOUT.

END OF ROUND SIX

ROUND SEVEN
Control Room

REF: *Still lying down.* Why are you still here? Afraid of blood?

MINA: The contemplation of ruins is a masculine specialty.

REF: I hope Geno's okay. I mean—he's not a bad guy.

MINA: Are you always going to back the underdog?

REF: Who are you for?

MINA: No one. I don't care.

REF: You must care about something.

MINA: I used to. But—

REF: What happened?

MINA: *Begins whispering, increases volume gradually.* It's not worth the effort. The eyes are too easy to close . . . I remember—last night or last year—a celebration . . . it was . . . a birthday, a birth, a day . . . something . . . important. We felt like children . . . we toasted the future—To Permanent Bliss—GULP!—AHH! We were infected. We gave our virus to anyone willing to spring for a round. . . . Drank free all night! . . . But . . . I had to leave . . . I needed something . . . I forgot. The cabs were full. . . . I walked . . . in the fog. Halfway home I stopped by this young tree. Planted by Friends of the Urban Forest! I don't know why, but I suddenly felt nauseous. I threw up on the spot. Looking up, I saw that sign of hope dripping puke as a tree died of thirst. I laughed so hard my wisdom teeth woke up. My mouth became swollen with pain. Blood and bile don't mix. They only trade places. The poison settles. You can't sleep a wink. All that planning and suddenly hibernation's out of the question. Asleep you need nothing . . . awake—forget it!—it's all about hunger. You remember a picnic— fresh fish and bread . . . well, fish anyway—the bakers are on strike . . . you leave the cave for the river and get lost in the snow—driven by pain you continue . . . no turning back till spring . . . if you can hold on that long . . . I cannot help you. My mouth aches with infection of my own manufacture. I'm hungry and alive, filled with the pure white light of pain.

REF *stays quiet. Eyes closed.*

MINA: That's it. Close your eyes. Sleep if you can. Energy is always wasted. Are you comfortable? *Strokes* REF's *head.*

REF: *Suddenly.* What time is it? I got to introduce Geno! I'm supposed to be on stage. I'm late! *Exits.*

MINA: I've not only lived my life for nothing—I've told it for nothing. It's all over now. Again—for the last time.

SOUND: *Bell rings. Fade* LIGHTS.

END OF ROUND SEVEN

ROUND EIGHT
The Retrofied Forest

GENO *sits on bench sobbing. Enter* ART.

GENO: I know I'm not that bad. I try so hard at something I like doing. I dream of winning. I see myself being picked up, carried around. You know—like a boxer? Sometimes I see it in slow motion . . . *Sees* ART. Hey—leave me alone!

ART: Come on, you bum! It ain't over yet.

GENO: I know. But it hurts!

ART: You giving up?

GENO: No!

ART: You afraid? You callin' it quits?

GENO: No!

ART: You quit now, it's all over. Is that what you want?

GENO: What difference does it make to you? You'll win—isn't that what you want?

ART: There's no victory without a struggle. Everyone will think it was staged. They counted on you to do what they couldn't. If you give up, they'll kill you—

GENO: I'm not a fighter. I'm just a nightclub owner.

ART: You think they'll buy that? Once they've seen you fight, they won't let you be anything else. You're their hope!

GENO: I was—but look at me now! I mean—pink bandages? I look like a clown! They'll laugh at me!

ART: Goddamn it! I need you! Don't do this to me!

GENO: This isn't happening.

ART: What—you think this is just some kind of metaphor? Some kind of symbol? This is life, baby! This is a fight! If this was just a symbol, I'd say the hell with it! Let's go! *Grabs* GENO.

GENO: I don't want to . . . I can't . . .

ART: Get back out there and fight.

Exit. ART *dragging* GENO.

SOUND: *Bell rings.* BLACKOUT.

END OF ROUND EIGHT

ROUND NINE
Main Stage

REF *holds* GENO's *arm, dragging him to center stage.* GENO *tries to run away.*

REF: It's time again now for the main event. But first, let's welcome the man who's full of the punch you love. The man who keeps the dream disconnected, Geno!!

GENO *has clearly aged. He's a physical wreck, ready to crumble. Falls and is helped up by* REF. *The crowd roars, then hushes.* GENO *mumbles and grumbles.*

GENO: Hello . . . *Voice cracking.* I'm Geno's father. Geno is in the control booth, watching. I am not Geno. I'm Geno's father.

REF: *Whispering.* What are you doing? Stop lying!

GENO: Don't be fooled. You can see. I'm too old to be Geno. Geno's in the control booth.

REF: Tell the truth! You're in pain! Why deny it? That's what life's all about! You can't fool these people forever.

GENO: I'm Geno's father. Geno's in the control room.

REF: Don't believe him! Tell the truth!

GENO: I'm not Geno! I'm . . . *Collapses.*

REF: Get up you bum! Get up!

VOICEOVER *counts to nine.* SOUND: *Bell rings.* LIGHTS *rise brighter.*

END OF ROUND NINE

ROUND TEN
Main Stage

REF *is holding* GENO *on his feet. Enter* ART, *swinging a few punches.* MINA *moves in behind* ART.

ART: How's everyone doing out there? I'm Geno. Welcome to my club. Starting next Tuesday, I'm happy to announce, we're opening a VIP room for our special guests.

REF: *Gets up.* You're Geno!

GENO: He's Geno?

ART: I'm—

REF: Ladies and Gentlemen, the Dream Disconnector—Geno! I got some great ideas, boss—what time you wanna meet tomorrow?

GENO: Don't believe him!

ART: *Pulls out rulebook which is now a datebook. To* REF. Hmm . . . tomorrow night's out—I'm relaxing with Amber. Let's do lunch—leisurely—at your place? Just you and me.

REF: Fantastic! No problem! *Laughs.* Oh yeah—Amber's looking for you.

GENO: Bay shrimp!

ART: She'll find me—I ain't paid her yet.

GENO *reaches in pocket for wallet—it's empty.*

REF: *Hands wallet of cash to* ART. You left this in the Control Room.

ART: You're kidding! You take anything? Ha, ha—Thank God you found this before she did.

REF: It's all there. Count it—

GENO *looks up.* REF *looks back and forth.*

ART: You're a snake charmer, baby. . . . But never a swindler.

GENO *tries to stand.*

ART: 'Sup with him? *To* GENO. Hey—you got a badge?

REF: He don't need no badge—he's Geno's old man.

ART: I don't care if he's Jesus motherfuckin Christ, what I'm sayin' if you don't got an all-access pass—get out!

Enter AMBER *(*MINA *with piercings).*

AMBER: *Bumps into* GENO. Hey, dude—you seen Geno?

GENO: I'm not G—I'm G—I'm not—I am—Security . . . stop—

AMBER: *Laughs.* I get it—you're a clown—ha, ha—you're funny—

REF: There she is—right on schedule.

AMBER: *To* REF. Oh—hey Bryan! 'Sup? You found Geno yet?

REF: Your eyes closed? You sleeping or something? He's right here!

ART: I'm Geno—your boyfriend.

AMBER: No you're not.

REF: *(To* AMBER.*)* Come on—You whacked out?

ART: I certainly ain't your great-grandfather.

AMBER: Huh?

ART: You look like shit!

AMBER: Fuck you—

ART: No, I mean it. You feel bad?

AMBER: I don't feel nothin' . . .

GENO: No pain, no p— *Rising, starts stumbling toward* AMBER.

REF: *(To* AMBER.*)* You sound dead.

ART: *(To* REF.*)* Stop him.

AMBER: I'm broke.

GENO: *(To* AMBER.*)* Let's get a room.

REF: Your set sounded awful.

ART: You don't get a dime.

AMBER: We had a contract!

GENO: Nice people . . .

AMBER: Where's my dough?

ART: Art took it—

GENO: Can I breathe now?

AMBER: Who's Art?

REF: The cheapest—

ART: Projection—

GENO: It's me—

REF: Him again!

ART: I said, "I can!"

GENO: Believe me, it hurts.

AMBER: Stop fucking around.

REF: Tricks!

ART: New technology!

GENO: More time!

AMBER: Yeah, more time—I ain't got all night.

SOUND: *Intro music plays.*

VOICEOVER: And now, ladies and gentlemen . . . the first Virtual Resurrection on the West Coast—

ART: I'm ready.

AMBER: Wha—?

REF: You both know the rules. Let's have a clean fight!

GENO: More time!

AMBER: 'Sup with all that?

REF: Okay. Start fighting!

ART: Again—for the last time!

SOUND: *Bell rings. Sharp* BLACKOUT.

END OF ROUND TEN

and

THE END

JACK the RAPPER

A PLAY BY KATHI GEORGES

STARRING
PETER CARLAFTES
JEAN MAZZEI
JESSICA MIDI
IAN HIRSCH

MARILYN MONROE MEMORIAL THEATER
96 LAFAYETTE STREET / 11TH -12TH - HOWARD / 415-552-3034 / 9 PM

ILLUSTRATION BY TOM FOWLER

JACK THE RAPPER

A Play on Madness

Inspired by T. S. Eliot's Poem
"Rhapsody on a Windy Night"

Dedicated to
the transformation of horror into beauty

PRODUCTION NOTES:

THE INFAMOUS "JACK THE RIPPER," popular nickname of the serial killer who brutally murdered prostitutes in Whitechapel, London in 1888, has never been definitively identified, though innumerable author-sleuths have offered theories they claim are beyond reproach. No single theory has been able to stand the test of time. Every few years, another author-sleuth develops another theory on the Ripper's identity and, inevitably, discredits all previous theories as rubbish.

For creative artists including novelists, playwrights, screenwriters, and musicians, the Jack the Ripper murders offer a wealth of material with which to work. Nearly fifty novels have used the Ripper as their base; countless operas, musicals, and plays have been produced; Link Wray turned "Jack the Ripper" into a classic instrumental pop song that starts with an evil laugh and a woman's scream; films galore have been screened from Alfred Hitchcock's 1927 adaptation of novel and play *The Lodger* to 1979's time travelling pursuit *Time After Time*, to 2001's Johnny Depp vehicle *From Hell*. Add to that video games, websites, and yes, even a couple of apps, and one has what could be the ultimate source of speculation of any human act on record.

My interest in creating another Jack the Ripper play was modest, but it turned into a full-blown passion following a deep reading of T. S. Eliot's 1915 poem "Rhapsody On A Windy Night." Those words crept into my dreams and twisted in my idle moments. Regard the first intricate stanza:

> Twelve o'clock.
> Along the reaches of the street
> Held in a lunar synthesis,
> Whispering lunar incantations
> Dissolve the floors of memory
> And all its clear relations,
> Its divisions and precisions,
> Every street lamp that I pass
> Beats like a fatalistic drum,
> And through the spaces of the dark
> Midnight shakes the memory
> As a madman shakes a dead geranium.

Certainly, notable scholars have developed notable theories about the meaning of this poem. But the more I read "Rhapsody . . . ," the more I believed it possible that the poem was inspired by Jack the Ripper, with nods to French symbolist poet Jules Laforgue. But why would Eliot have any interest in writing a piece about such a low-life, trashy crime? What if there was a particular, specific connection between Eliot and the Ripper murders? Being receptive to all thoughts, I developed my theory, and found the perfect vehicle with which to deliver it by writing the play, *Jack the Rapper*.

In creating *Jack the Rapper*, I opted to make a play that would span three time periods: London's East End in 1888, the year the Ripper murders occurred; the Bedford Square, London drawing room of Lady Ottoline Morrell, noted aristocrat and frequent host of the Bloomsbury group circa 1917; and Los Angeles, circa 1999, at a venue hosting the first major appearance of up-and-coming pop star Jack the Rapper. Tying these disparate parts together in the "Dressing Womb" is Jack, an embryonic philosopher-artist, a collective memory of all things past, analyzing the necessity of birth in a world that would allow, nurture, and fixate on such gruesome violence. The play twists these multiple threads round and round into a frenzy that elicits the sensation of madness, interspersing sinister, shadowy scenes of Ripper murder suspects with modern day pop star image-makers; juxtaposing letters of the Ripper with Eliot's poem; matching serious philosophical musings against an ether-fueled Ezra Pound breaking into a subconscious chorus of multiple personas inhabiting his mind.

With multiple scene changes and nineteen characters, the play might seem like it was a bit overly-ambitious for the intimate confines of San Francisco's Marilyn Monroe Memorial Theater, where it premiered in 1999. But with the inventive set design of Peter Carlaftes, imaginative video and audio tracks, plus a resourceful cast of four (Carlaftes, Jean Mazzei, Ian Hirsch, and Jessica Midi) playing multiple roles, the play came off magnificently.

So, herein, I present *Jack the Rapper*. Let the madness begin and may it result in further inspiration and creation—a cure for the destruction and brutality from whence it came.

—*K. G.*

JACK THE RAPPER
A Play on Madness
by Kat Georges

CHARACTERS

LATE TWENTIETH-CENTURY CHARACTERS

JACK
a foetus with a past, waiting to be born
current home: The Dressing Womb

ANNIE
a woman full of secrets.
as ANNIE CROOK: *secret lover of Prince Albert "*EDDY*" Victor*
as ANNIE DUNNE: *beloved nanny of* T. S. ELIOT
as ANNIE: *modern-day prostitute; ether addict; victim of Jack the Rapper*

STEPHEN
a bully of a man; macho pop start marketing master; business partner of
    WENDY KNIGHT *to whom he is secretly married; suspect in Jack the*
    Rapper murder case
as STEPHEN WHITE: *Inspector with Metropolitan Police Whitechapel*
    division; suspect in Jack the Ripper murder case; in 1999 lives in
    STEPHEN'*s head*

WENDY
manipulative, power-driven pop starmaker; business partner of and secretly
    married to STEPHEN; *pregnant with* JACK; *agent and manager of pop*
    sensation JACK THE RAPPER

LATE NINETEENTH-CENTURY LONDON CHARACTERS

INDIAN HARRY
slumlord in late nineteenth-century Whitechapel, London; owner of the apartment complex lived in by MARY JANE KELLY *and* CATHERINE PICKETT

MARY JANE KELLY
prostitute in late nineteenth-century Whitechapel, London. Lives in room rented from slumlord INDIAN HARRY. *Final confirmed victim of Jack the Ripper*

GEORGE HUTCHINSON
witness and suspect in Jack the Ripper case; gave detailed description of man he saw outside MARY JANE KELLY*'s room. Too detailed.*

MONTAGUE DRUITT
barrister, teacher, and suspect in Jack the Ripper case

CATHERINE PICKETT
nineteenth-century flower seller; witness in Jack the Ripper case (never called to testify); lived in same apartment complex as MARY JANE KELLY; *heard her singing "A Violet from Mother's Grave" loudly on the night of her murder.*

PRINCE ALBERT "EDDY" VICTOR
Son of Prince Albert Edward and Princess Alexandra. Heir to the throne; secretly married to ANNIE CROOK.

EARLY TWENTIETH-CENTURY LONDON CHARACTERS

LADY OTTOLINE MORRELL
London aristocrat and society hostess. Regular hostess and patron of the Bloomsbury Group, including T. S. ELIOT *(and wife,* VIVIENNE*) and* EZRA POUND.

EZRA POUND
The poet himself; herein a carrier of many spirits of the past including EDDY, APPOLLINAIRE, DRUITT, STEPHEN WHITE

T. S. ELIOT
The poet himself; herein nursing an infatuation with the mystery of the identity of Jack the Ripper

VIVIENNE HAIGH-WOOD ELIOT
T. S. ELIOT*'s wife; pretty, ambitious, fragile health, but otherwise vivacious, ether addict*

SETTINGS

DRESSING WOMB / BACKSTAGE

A womb-shaped container, red and pink, plush and lit from within, open in the front; inhabited by JACK; *equipped with a loud buzzer that marks the time. The area outside of the Dressing Womb is Backstage at huge first 1999 Los Angeles concert for pop star Jack the Rapper.*

OUTISIDE LOS ANGELES BAR, 1999

A high-end tavern for hip people and their takers; lit in front by a street lamp.

OUTSIDE WHITECHAPEL LONDON PUB, 1888

A low-end tavern for down-and-outers and their makers; lit in front by a street lamp.

LADY OTTOLINE MORRELL'S DRAWING ROOM, 1917

A plush room of overstuffed chairs and paintings ruled by its owner; herein visited during times of World War I air raids

MENTAL ASYLUM NEW MEXICO, 1999

Place where Stephen White hides after becoming a suspect in the Jack the Rapper murder

ST. LOUIS, MISSOURI HOME, 1910

Birthplace of T. S. Eliot, where he returned briefly before moving to France

PRELUDE
Dressing Womb
Los Angeles, 1999
Twelve o'clock

JACK: In my beginning is my end.

Fade LIGHTS *up*

JACK: It wasn't my idea to begin. I'm here because—

Loud buzz. JACK *twitches.*

JACK: Who cares? Someone does. . . . Well. . . . Someone did. It's a
secret. *Pause.* That's a clue—*whispers.*

Fade out LIGHTS *on* JACK.

SCENE I
Outside Bar
Los Angeles, 1999
Twelve o'clock

ANNIE *strikes a hooker pose near the front door of a bar.* STEPHEN *exits bar on video enters stage talking on cell phone to* WENDY, *who, unknown to him, is inside the same bar he just left.*

ANNIE: Got a light?

STEPHEN: *(To cell phone.)* What's that?

ANNIE: A light?

STEPHEN: *Annoyed.* I quit.

ANNIE: Oh well.

She moves away and stands near street lamp.

STEPHEN: *(To cell phone.)* What? . . . No—Fed Ex— . . . I'm at the office. You know me. A working stiff. *(To Annie.)* Don't go. *(To cell phone.)* Really. How's London? . . . *Panic.* What? . . . Oh, shit. You're back. Where are you now?

WENDY: Turn around. STEPHEN *turns.* WENDY *puts cell phone away.*

STEPHEN: *(To cell phone.)* Holy cow! I can explain.

WENDY: No you can't.

STEPHEN: Don't hang up. *Smiles sheepishly.* Oh. *Puts cell phone away.* Wendy! Boy, we missed you. How'd it go?

WENDY: Cut the crap.

STEPHEN: No, really. Who'd you sign? The next big thing? Tell me, tell me.

WENDY: No.

STEPHEN: Please . . .

Pause

WENDY: Two acts.

STEPHEN: That's it? Shit. Musicians?

WENDY: Models.

STEPHEN: Not again.

WENDY: Musicians don't need us, Stephen. They got the fucking Internet. And these punks, these two-bit shit bands, Christ! They're getting rich without our help. The little snots invest in stocks—they leave the rest to lawyers. Lawyers—God, they all have lawyers—shit—I talked to twenty-one of them, tried to cut a deal. Oh, well. London lawyers know two words. All I heard was "fuck" and "you."

STEPHEN: What'd you do?

WENDY: I went direct. Hid backstage. Turned on the charm. Tried my luck. Finally got to talk to a lead singer.

STEPHEN: What band?

WENDY: The Schmucks! I tell him, let me sign you up. You're big in Chiswick now—so what? You want big bucks? Think "America." He says—USA? They know us there. I say—Got proof? I bloody do, he says. And then—oh, God—I almost puke. He pulls his little laptop out—gets his little website up—grins his stupid little grin—and says—"We've got four million fans." CDs, groupies— all online. And we don't make a fucking dime.

STEPHEN: Online groupies?

WENDY: I kid you not. These guys call them, chat-room sluts. I tell you, Stephen, the whole thing sucks. It's so wrong.

STEPHEN: You've been in this business too long.

WENDY: Excuse me for venting.

STEPHEN: You're the boss. Well, for now.

WENDY: You ain't getting my job.

STEPHEN: Things change. There's been talk—

WENDY: Oh? What's going on?

STEPHEN: I can't say a word.

WENDY: Aren't you . . . due for a raise?

STEPHEN: Overdue.

WENDY: Tell you what— You help me, I help you.

STEPHEN: Money talks.

WENDY: Understood. These two acts from London. Models. Real cute. They look great on TV. That's worth . . . two hits apiece. You write—I produce—you get three points of profit—

STEPHEN: Sounds good.

WENDY: Let's talk in six months. Seven tops.

ANNIE *moves next to* STEPHEN *and smiles sexily.*

STEPHEN: *Hands keys to Annie.* Green Jag. Back lot.

WENDY: Who's your friend?

STEPHEN: Who—her? Valet.

WENDY: Some girl . . .

STEPHEN: Not my type. Now, Wen—

ANNIE: *(To* WENDY, *in a flirtatious voice.)* My name's Annie

STEPHEN: What about—

ANNIE *exits.*

WENDY: Wait here. *Exits.*

STEPHEN: —my raise?

WENDY: *Offstage.* Sorry. *Yells.* Annie!

STEPHEN: I quit. *Calls a mysterious someone on cell phone.*

WENDY: *Offstage.* What?

STEPHEN: *(To Wendy.)* I said— *(To cell phone.)* Hurry up, please. It's time. *(To Wendy.)* I quit. *(To cell phone.)* Do her in.

WENDY: *Offstage.* You can't quit.

STEPHEN: *(To Wendy.)* Hold on. *(To cell phone.)* *Angry.* Look— You'll get paid! . . . Yeah . . . *(To Wendy.)* You heard me. *(To cell phone.)* Just call me when you're done.

Hangs up.

Cell phone rings.

STEPHEN: That was quick. *Answers cell phone.* This is Stephen . . . —

WENDY: *Voice on phone.* I'll double your salary. Triple your stock. Just tell me what's up.

STEPHEN: Are you serious?

WENDY: *Voice on phone.* Yes.

STEPHEN: Fuck. *(To cell phone.)* We got a deal, Wendy. *Aside.* Oh shit. *(To cell phone.)* Hold on . . . *Calls another number on cell phone.* Hello? Umm . . . Change of plans. . . —It's too late? No it's not. . . . Yes. I'm talking to her—Yes. Hang on. *Switches line.* Wendy—you there? . . . Hello? Hello? *Scream. Dial tone. Switches lines.* Shit. What the hell's going on? Hello? Hello? *Dial tone.* Fuck!

WENDY: *Entering.* Okay talk—What's up? Buy-out? Takeover? Merge? Tell me the truth—How come they're keeping me out of the loop? *Pause.* You're not talking. Whose side are you on?

STEPHEN *puts phone away.*

STEPHEN: You're alive . . . uh-oh. Where's that girl?

WENDY: Annie? She split.

STEPHEN: Holy shit.

Begins exiting.

WENDY: Get back here or no deal.

STEPHEN: I get that raise—or I walk. I got an offer. Mega-bucks.

WENDY: You whore.

STEPHEN: Says who?

WENDY: Your boss.

STEPHEN: My pimp.

WENDY: Your wife.

STEPHEN: Tell your girlfriend.

WENDY: I'm straight. Since June.

STEPHEN: Me, too.

WENDY: You?

STEPHEN: Since July twenty-two.

WENDY: *Hugs* STEPHEN. Oh, Stephen.

STEPHEN: Oh, babe. . . .

WENDY: *Stern.* Stephen. Don't cry.

Pause.

STEPHEN: I love you.

WENDY: Me too.

They kiss a long time.

VOICEOVER ANNOUNCEMENT: If the lady and gentleman wish to take their tea in the garden, if the lady and gentleman wish to take their tea in the garden . . .

Tender, starry-eyed, schmaltzy moment. Pause.

WENDY: Remember our honeymoon?

STEPHEN: Just like a dream. Champagne and romance. Paris, London, Berlin . . . —

WENDY: We never left Vegas. You almost OD'd.

STEPHEN: Champagne?

WENDY: Percodan, peyote, and speed. *Pause.* Remember the hotel in London, Las Vegas? The Sperm Bank Hotel?

STEPHEN: Let's go back.

WENDY: It's not real. But the fake one inspired a real one to be built.

STEPHEN: Where?

WENDY: In London, of course. Real London.

STEPHEN: I'm there.

WENDY: Well, you were.

STEPHEN: Huh?

WENDY: I saw you—well, not exactly—I saw your—you know—

STEPHEN: My sperm?

WENDY: Yes. Guess what? You were on sale—half-price. So I bought you. . . . —

STEPHEN: Half-price? My sperm? Me?

WENDY: Yes, and well . . .

STEPHEN: Well what, Wendy?

WENDY: I'm pregnant.

Pause.

STEPHEN: Taxi! *Exits.* Wait! My car!

WENDY: It's yours. *(To cell phone.)* All set?

STEPHEN: *Offstage.* Fuck my car.

WENDY: *(To cell phone.)* Make it real. Roll tape . . . mark it. Cue lights. *Blackout.* Monitor. *TV on.* Cue sound. ACTION!

END OF SCENE I

INTERLUDE
Video

VIDEO SOUND: Twelve o'clock. Along the reaches of the street / Held in a lunar synthesis / Whispering lunar incantations / Dissolve the floors of memory / And all its clear relations / Its division and precisions / Every streetlamp that I pass / Beats like a fatalistic drum / And through the spaces of the dark / Midnight shakes the memory / As a madman shakes a dead geranium.

VIDEO SCENE: *Front of bar from Scene I.* STEPHEN *paces in front, waiting for* ANNIE *to return with his car.*

CUT TO *Taxi.* POV *Passenger (*JACK*). Passing neon lights and hookers. pulls into bar parking lot.* CLOSE UP *of* STEPHEN*'s car.* JACK *gets out of cab. Cab pulls away.*

CUT TO STEPHEN *flagging down cab.*

CUT TO *bar parking lot.* CLOSE UP *of keys on ground next to* STEPHEN*'s car.* JACK *sees them and picks them up.*

CUT TO *car.* JACK *approaches. Tries key on door—it fits. Begins to open door.*

CUT TO STEPHEN *getting into cab. Cab pulls into bar parking lot* STEPHEN *sees* JACK *opening door to his car.* STEPHEN *jumps out of cab and runs toward* JACK.

CUT TO *car door opening.* ANNIE *(dead) falls out with knife sticking out of her chest.*

CUT TO STEPHEN *running.*

CUT TO *knife, in* JACK*'s hand.*

CUT TO STEPHEN *running.*

CUT TO JACK's *hand. Knife falls out.* JACK *runs away.*

CUT TO STEPHEN. *Picks up knife. Shakes* ANNIE.

STEPHEN: *(on video, screams)* Murder!! Help!! Murder!!! Help me!!

SCENE II
Dressing Womb
Los Angeles, 1999

VOICE: Hurry up, please. It's time.

JACK: *In womb.* Ever since I got here, I have the strangest dreams. Every time I close my eyes, I remember bits and pieces. The truth is—I don't know if in fact what I remember is really a dream. How can anyone dream of people and places he's never seen? How can anyone dream of agony unless they've known it before—lived through it firsthand. Maybe I have . . . In my beginning . . .

SOUND: *Loud buzz.* JACK *twitches.*

JACK: They watch me like a hawk. Who knows what they'll do? *Whisper.* One slip and I'm out of here. This time for good.

SOUND: *Loud buzz.* JACK *twitches.*

JACK: I mean, I got to use words when I talk to you. See? I can't ever say what I mean.

ANNIE *appears.*

JACK: Greetings.

ANNIE: Hello.

JACK: I'm Jack.

ANNIE: Is that so?

VOICE: Hurry up, please. It's time.

JACK: You remind me of someone I used to know.

ANNIE: Who?

JACK: If I tell you, you'll laugh. *Pause.* You remind me of you. You're not laughing. You're . . . crying? It's a compliment, really.

ANNIE: I think it's lovely.

JACK: It's the best lie I've got.

VOICE: Hurry up, please. It's time.

Pause.

JACK: Are you hungry?

ANNIE: No.

JACK: I don't mean to be rude, but . . . *Eats.* . . . There's plenty of food.

ANNIE: You need food. I need you. You'll have to leave here soon.

JACK: What's that? In your hand?

ANNIE: A rose.

JACK: Doesn't smell like a rose.

ANNIE: It's paper.

JACK: It's yours?

ANNIE: You bought it for me.

JACK: Impossible!

ANNIE: Did you forget?

JACK: Look here, miss—

ANNIE: You bought it out there. When you had money. Out there. You can have it again.

JACK: I got it all here. I can eat, sleep, and dream.

ANNIE: I think I'd be bored.

VOICE: Hurry up, please. It's time.

ANNIE: Are you . . . bored?

JACK: Me? Nah . . .

ANNIE: How do you know?

VOICE: Hurry up, please. It's time.

JACK: I've been out there before.

SOUND: *Loud buzz.* JACK *twitches.*

JACK: Are you hungry?

ANNIE: No. Why do you keep asking me?

JACK: Killing time.

ANNIE: Nothing's changed.

JACK: *Whispers.* Do you know where I am? . . . I mean—is this—heaven or hell?

ANNIE: It's L.A. We're backstage. The show's about to begin.

JACK: Who's performing?

ANNIE: You are.

JACK: Oh, God. Not again.

SOUND: *Loud buzz.* JACK *twitches.*

JACK: This is the way the world ends.

ANNIE: Do you remember how it began?

VOICE: Hurry up, please it's time.

JACK: Time for this. *Turns on TV.*

BLACKOUT.

END OF SCENE II

INTERLUDE
Video

TV INTERVIEWER: Okay, Wendy. Tell us—who's Jack?

TV WENDY KNIGHT: Don't ask me. If I knew, I would—natural—tell the police.

TV INTERVIEWER: Did you talk to the police yet?

TV WENDY KNIGHT: Talk about torture. Thank God for my lawyers—

Shot of lawyer sitting next to WENDY.

TV LAWYER: Fuck you.

TV WENDY KNIGHT: London.

TV INTERVIEWER: Poser. *Pause.* Is Jack the Ripper a lawyer?

TV LAWYER: Fuck you.

TV WENDY KNIGHT: Don't ask me. *Exits.*

TV INTERVIEWER: I mean, Jack the Rapper . . . — *Pause.* Play the goddamn CD.

TV off.

AUDIO: *Jack the Rapper (hip hop version of "Rhapsody on a Windy Night")*

SCENE III
Outside Pub
Whitechapel, London, 1888
Half-past one.

INDIAN HARRY: *In dark.* What do say, sailor? Helluva whore, see? *Pause.* Aww, hell.

LIGHTS: *Street lamp fades up.*

INDIAN HARRY: *Yells at person who just passed by in dark.* Ye's a fairy!

MARY JANE: Or killer.

INDIAN HARRY: Not he. Tha's a fairy whore, Kelly.

MARY JANE: 'Ow 'a 'hell d'ye know? Are ye a owin' 'im, 'Harry. *Laughs.*

INDIAN HARRY: Yer the one 'oo's owin', Kelly. . . . Three months rent.

MARY JANE: I know, I know.

INDIAN HARRY: Thirty-three shillings.

MARY JANE: I know, I know.

INDIAN HARRY: An' Joe say he wants it tomorrow, eh?

MARY JANE: I'll 'ave it, I te' ye.

INDIAN HARRY: Ye'll drink it away. *Pause.* Whore! Hella whore, see? *Pause.* . . . 'Nother fairy.

MARY JANE: Yer scarin' 'em off, 'Arry. Why'n't ye 'ead 'ome? I'll make me money in no time, and—

INDIAN HARRY: Spend it on rum.

MARY JANE: I mi' 'ave a sip—

INDIAN HARRY: Ye've been sippin' already. Ye 'ad a cup in Ten Bells—

MARY JANE: 'At were bot fer me, 'Arry.

INDIAN HARRY: *Yells.* Whore for sale, whore!

MARY JANE: 'At's a cop.

INDIAN HARRY: *Peers.* Tis? Sorry. *Yells.* Never mind, sor. *(To* MARY.*)* Least 'e isn't th' Ripper.

MARY JANE: 'Oo knows?

INDIAN HARRY: There's that fairy again.

MARY JANE: 'Arry . . . Go home. I'll have yer rent in the morning.

INDIAN HARRY: Joe wants it first thing. I'll pop by at seven.

MARY JANE: Pop by at eleven.

INDIAN HARRY: 'At's up to Joe, lass.

MARY JANE: I 'ave to 'ave sleep. Make it ten and—*Feels* HARRY'*s crotch. Seductive.*

INDIAN HARRY: I'll ask.

MARY JANE: *Calls out.* Mr. Hutchinson! *(To* INDIAN HARRY.*)* Thanks, 'Arry. You're very kind. *Exiting.* See you at ten.

INDIAN HARRY: But Joe said—

MARY JANE: Change his mind.

BLACKOUT.

Later, Outside Same Pub
Whitechapel, London, 1888
Half-past two.

In BLACKOUT.

MARY JANE'S VOICE: Misher Hushinsan!

HUTCHINSON'S VOICE: Kelly, lass, why are ye out? It's 'alf past one, here—and tis rainin' now—

MARY JANE'S VOICE: Sor. Ca' ye len' me a si'pence?

HUTCHINSON'S VOICE: I'm broke.

MARY JANE'S VOICE: 'At's a shame.

HUTCHINSON'S VOICE: Lost me job, and me wife is with child again. Thirteen children already, and all under ten. And all sick as could be, like me wife, me mum too—

MARY JANE'S VOICE: Misher Hushinson?

HUTCHINSON'S VOICE: Yes?

MARY JANE'S VOICE: I don't believe you.

HUTCHINSON'S VOICE: Ach. I am broke—spent me day at the track. But I was hopin'—

MARY JANE'S VOICE: Not tonight.

DRUITT'S VOICE: *Breathless.* Kelly!

HUTCHINSON'S VOICE: I'll pay ye back.

MARY JANE'S VOICE: Sorry.

DRUITT'S VOICE: Kelly!

HUTCHINSON'S VOICE: Good morning, then.

MARY JANE'S VOICE: Good morning. I must go and find some money.

Pause. Sound of walking footsteps fading. Sound of running footsteps approaching.

DRUITT'S VOICE: *Breathless.* Kelly! Mary Jane!

LIGHTS *up.*

DRUITT'S VOICE: Kelly!

Enter DRUITT. MARY JANE *hides in shadows.*

DRUITT: Mary Jane! . . .

MARY JANE: Psst . . . Mister—

DRUITT: Kelly? Is that you?

MARY JANE: 'Oo wants to know?

DRUITT: I do.

MARY JANE: Oh, ye do? Might I ask—'oo are you?

DRUITT: Montague Druitt.

MARY JANE: MD.

DRUITT: Call me John.

MARY JANE: You a doctor?

DRUITT: Uh, no. Barrister. Teacher.

MARY JANE: Stand in the light. Let's see ye— . . . Oh me God! *Steps out of shadows.* Ye look just like—

DRUITT: The Duke.

MARY JANE: The Duke . . .—'Aay—'Ow'd ye know that?

DRUITT: I know Eddy.

MARY JANE: Ye do? Is 'at a fact?

DRUITT: It is. You see, Eddy and I used to . . . —

MARY JANE: What?

DRUITT: Never mind. Are you Mary Jane Kelly?

MARY JANE: I've seen you haven't I . . . —

DRUITT: Are you Kelly?

MARY JANE: Aye. I remember. I seen ye before. You're a fairy whore, aren't ye. 'Arry told me ye were. I said, 'Ow ye know, 'Arry? Ye owin' him? You know Harry. He says—

DRUITT: Who's Harry?

MARY JANE: Indian Harry.

DRUITT: I'm afraid—

MARY JANE: His real name is Tom. Works for McArthy. Real dick of a man. Hey! Tom, Dick, and Harry—*Laughs*—All wrapped up in one.

DRUITT: *Wanders off.* Kelly! Mary Jane!

MARY JANE: Hey Mister, John—come back.

DRUITT: I have to find her.

MARY JANE: Well . . . ye 'ave.

DRUITT: You sure?

MARY JANE: I ought to know my own name, sor. But with the Ripper on the prowl—

DRUITT: I understand.

Pause.

MARY JANE: Hey—You aren't—

DRUITT: No.

MARY JANE: Then what ye want me for, sor?

DRUITT: Well . . . It's a long story.

MARY JANE: *In street lamp light.* Sure it is. Look, i' ye want me, ye pay for me services, see?

DRUITT: I'm a fairy, remember?

Pause.

MARY JANE: 'Ow well ye know Eddy?

DRUITT: That's a long story, too.

MARY JANE: 'E's married, ye know?

DRUITT: Not so loud.

MARY JANE: Did ye know—

DRUITT: *Covers* MARY JANE's *mouth.* I know everything.

MARY JANE: *Pulling* DRUITT's *hand off her mouth.* Ye don't know me. Not at all.

DRUITT: You want to die?

MARY JANE: Maybe. Why?

DRUITT: The Ripper's out for blood tonight.

MARY JANE: What the 'ell ye waiting for?

DRUITT: I'm—

CATHERINE: *Offstage.* Flowers!

DRUITT: *Whispers.* —Not the Ripper.

MARY JANE: Oh, sure. Mister—look—I 'ave to make me rent by the morn. See? If ye want—do me in, that's fine by me. Otherwise— leave.

DRUITT: You're with child, aren't you?

MARY JANE: Umm . . . Maybe.

Enter CATHERINE.

CATHERINE: Flowwwers!

MARY JANE: Buy me a rose.

CATHERINE: Flowers! Roses! All fresh . . . sort o'. A rose for ye, sire?
  Sees MARY JANE. What da' hell's this? Kelly!

MARY JANE: *(To* DRUITT.*)* I want a rose. A red rose.

CATHERINE: *(To* DRUITT.*)* A red rose?

DRUITT: I suppose.

Reaches for wallet.

CATHERINE: *(To* DRUITT.*)* Eight ye owe. *(To* MARY JANE.*)* So, Kelly,
  what's this? Whorin' is ye? Ah, lass— . . . Tis a devil ye is—*(To*
  DRUITT.*)* Ye owe eight. *(To* MARY JANE.*)*—What with that madman
  a-roamin' the streets . . . just a longing to reach one such as
  yourself—*(To* DRUITT.*)* Sir? —The eight? *(To* MARY JANE.*)* Heard
  you're with child.

MARY JANE: Aye, that I am.

CATHERINE: This the father, then?

DRUITT: Umm . . . Yes, yes.

CATHERINE: *Whisper to* MARY JANE. Are ye sure?

MARY JANE: Catherine!

DRUITT: Here's the eight.

CATHERINE: Here's yer rose.

DRUITT: Mary Jane?

MARY JANE: Thank you, John.

CATHERINE: John? That's his name?

MARY JANE: Mmm-hmm. Montague John, uh—

DRUITT: Druitt.

MARY JANE: Montague Druitt. MD. Like a doctor.

CATHERINE: Is he?

MARY JANE: Oh, yes.

DRUITT: Actually, I'm a barrister. And a teacher.

CATHERINE: I see. Ow! Ye know—ye look just like Eddy—

MARY JANE: *Cuts her off.* Honey! Look at this rose! It's paper, bejesus.

DRUITT: What's the meaning of this?

CATHERINE: A paper rose, sor, will always look fresh. Look at these. Fresh just this morning, now they're dead.

DRUITT: Nothing's dead—except what does not yet exist—Like a baby—

CATHERINE: These are dead—

MARY JANE: Not yet—

CATHERINE: You want it?

DRUITT: Do you?

MARY JANE: *Pause.* Sure.

DRUITT: *Hands tip to* CATHERINE. Thank you. Good-night.

CATHERINE: Floowers! *Exits.* Flowers! Roses! All fresh! Sort of.

DRUITT: Who *is* the father?

MARY JANE: Could be a copper . . .

DRUITT: Stephen White?

MARY JANE: *Pause.* 'Ow'd you know?

DRUITT: I know everything.

MARY JANE: Hell—What's a barrister like you doing in Whitechapel, London, at half past two in the morning outside in the rain?

DRUITT: Don't ask.

MARY JANE: Come on. *Pause.* I'll tell Steven White. He's that copper, you know. I'll tell him you tried to do me in. . . . I'll tell him. I will. *Pause.* What do you want?

DRUITT: I can't tell you here.

MARY JANE: Look—buy a bucket of beer and let's go to my room. You'll be comfortable there. May as well get off the street while we can. I'll build us a fire. You look cold.

DRUITT: *Coldly.* I am.

MARY JANE: You see? I insist. There's a pub just ahead. If you like— I'll run in—fetch the beer—I don't mind. Stay here—

DRUITT: I'll go with you.

MARY JANE: Now, John—don't bother—I'll be fine. Look here's my key—take it—go on—Miller's Court—room thirteen—Ta-Ta. Oh—dear me. I forgot. I've no money. Have you, John?

DRUITT: I do.

MARY JANE: How much you got?

DRUITT: Enough.

MARY JANE: My God!

DRUITT: This is for beer. And this—is for you. Thirty-three shillings. Eddy sends his regards.

MARY JANE: How is Eddy?

DRUITT: I'm fine. I mean—he's fine. Eddy.

MARY JANE: So it is you!

DRUITT: I'm John.

MARY JANE: Of course you are.

DRUITT: Mary Jane. Can't you see? You're in grave danger. You saw Eddy get married.

MARY JANE: Oh, that.

DRUITT: You know Eddy's wife.

MARY JANE: Annie?

DRUITT: And his son—that's why White—

MARY JANE: She has a son? Uh . . . What's his name?

DRUITT: You're to leave London tonight.

MARY JANE: What's all this talk about Steven White? Honestly. He's a little rough, otherwise.

DRUITT: He's insane.

MARY JANE: Who isn't these days? And why should I trust you?

DRUITT: I bought you a rose.

MARY JANE: It's paper.

DRUITT: It's yours.

MARY JANE: *Twists rose, eyes closed. Softly, sadly, starts to sing.* It was only a violet I plucked from my mother's grave as a boy. . . .

Fade to BLACKOUT.

END OF SCENE III

INTERLUDE
Audio

Quick sound bytes heard as channels change on TV

AUDIO: Who is Jack the Rapper? . . . Jack the Rapper has struck
again . . . The macabre and mysterious murderer Jack the
Rapper . . . Police still have no leads on the identity of Jack the
Rapper. . . . Jacques le Rapier c'est mordre . . . Number one on the
charts for the eleventh consecutive week—Jack the . . . I think it's
disgusting. . . . knife control advocates . . . He cuts just like a sushi
chef. . . . No more sushi! . . . Y2K . . . He must be a foreigner . . .
The profile suggests he is well-educated, probably drives a nice
car . . . We have no leads at this time . . . Mr. Mayor—what action
are you taking to stop this lunatic . . . No. 1 on the charts . . . Jack
the— . . . I think it's disgusting . . . In a bizarre twist— . . . A
concert? . . . Tickets at all major . . . I think it's disgusting . . . The
show sold out in under a minute . . . Who is Jack the Rapper . . .
Who was Jack the Ripper . . . Are they related? . . . The experts
say . . . —

SCENE IV
Ottoline Morrell's Drawing Room
Bedford Square, England, 1917

OTTOLINE MORRELL, EZRA POUND, VIVIENNE HAIGH-WOOD ELIOT *and*
T. S. ELIOT are seated comfortably, sipping drinks. VIVIENNE
occasionally inhales from a small vial of ether.

OTTOLINE: Jack the Ripper had a son? That's a laugh. He wasn't
born. His father killed him in the womb. And then, thank God,
he killed himself—at least, that's what the papers say.

VIVIENNE: Who was the Ripper anyway?

ELIOT: *(To* OTTOLINE.*)* She doesn't read the papers.

OTTOLINE *laughs.*

EZRA: Ha.

VIVIENNE: Don't laugh. I read—

EZRA: *Holds up palms.* Read these . . .—

OTTOLINE: He was a teacher.

VIVIENNE: Ask Tom—

OTTOLINE: Please.

EZRA: And a barrister—

ELIOT: And *The Lodger.*

EZRA: *Groans.* Dreadful play.

OTTOLINE: Anyhow—Jack the Ripper. *Irritated.* —was a barrister. Passed the bar, put up a shingle—

EZRA: *As if reading a sign.* JACK – THE – RIPPER, Helluva Barrister.

OTTOLINE: A barrister he was.

ELIOT: In the *Times*, anyway.

OTTOLINE: And for your information, he used his real name—uh— Montague John, uh—

EZRA: Druitt.

OTTOLINE: Yes, Pound.

ELIOT: You're well informed. Do you read?

EZRA: Only these. *Holds up hands.*

ELIOT: *Holds out hands.* You prefer left or right?

EZRA: I . . . right.

ELIOT: So do I.

EZRA: *Aside to* ELIOT. I get paid. So should you.

ELIOT: By whom?

EZRA: Ottoline? This man needs a patron.

OTTOLINE: I'm telling a story, Pound. May I continue?

EZRA: Absolutely. By all means. Continue. Go on— Please, go on. *Pause.* Ottoline? *Pause.* Ottoline?

Pause. OTTOLINE *almost begins to speak.*

VIVIENNE: *Suddenly.* Tom reads the papers every Sunday. *Laughs. No one else laughs.*

ELIOT: Ottoline?

OTTOLINE: May I?

ELIOT: Please.

Pause.

OTTOLINE: Jack the Ripper—

EZRA: John.

OTTOLINE: Yes, yes. So, Jack the—

EZRA: John—

OTTOLINE: The Jack—

EZRA: The John.

OTTOLINE: *(To* ELIOT.*)* Your turn.

ELIOT: *(To* EZRA.*)* I pass to Ezra.

EZRA: Thank you, sir. The truth is Jack is John, as such—the story is—

OTTOLINE: *Fills glass of* ELIOT. Feel free to interrupt. EZRA *holds up glass. (To* EZRA.) Go on.

Pause. EZRA *puts down glass.*

EZRA: Thanks a lot. Montague John, uh—

VIVIENNE: Druitt.

EZRA: Correct.

OTTOLINE: You remember.

VIVIENNE: Of course.

ELIOT: Clap-trap mind. *Laughs.*

EZRA: Ha.

ELIOT: Sometimes.

VIVIENNE: Show respect, dear.

ELIOT: Yes, dear.

EZRA: *(To* OTTOLINE.) Where's my check, dear?

OTTOLINE: Oh, dear. I don't have it here.

EZRA: So Montague John—

ELIOT: Druitt.

VIVIENNE: *(To* EZRA.) Go on—

ELIOT: Is it true that—

VIVIENNE: *(To* ELIOT.*)* Quiet.

EZRA: He went to Oxford. So did I. So did Tom.

OTTOLINE: You went to Oxford?

VIVIENNE: And Harvard.

EZRA: Did you? Me too. Bright young man—rosy future. And then—

ELIOT: *(To* VIVIENNE.*)* I married you.

Silence. VIVIENNE *and* ELIOT *stare at each other.*

EZRA: His father had a heart attack. . . . His mother cracked. His business failed. And dear old Jack—er, John—bought a knife, a long, sharp knife . . . and—no doubt—a map—

ELIOT: Of course—

EZRA: He must have had a map—

ELIOT: A Baedecker—

EZRA: Well . . . perhaps. And then—

OTTOLINE: Chop, chop—

EZRA: Chop, chop?

OTTOLINE: I'm bored.

EZRA: Carry on, Tom.

OTTOLINE: Eliot? The story is yours.

Pause.

ELIOT: How should I begin?

OTTOLINE: Chop, chop.

ELIOT: The end.

OTTOLINE: Thank you, good man. We saw *The Lodger.*

EZRA: Dreadful play.

OTTOLINE: And, with this war—who needs more horror? I think—

VIVIENNE: *Seriously.* It's awful. People are dying.

Pause.

OTTOLINE *and* VIVIENNE *speak over* EZRA *and* ELIOT*'s conversation.* EZRA
wants another drink and tries to work his way over to OTTOLINE, *and
the bottle she holds.* VIVIENNE *hides from* ELIOT*'s eyes.* OTTOLINE *uses*
ELIOT *as a shield to keep* EZRA *away.*

OTTOLINE: I think— The second this war ends, the new Britain
begins. Look at France. Look at Russia. We can and should learn
from others. Within the ruling classes themselves, a foreboding
is dawning, that the present society is no solid crystal, but an
organism capable of change, and one that is constantly changing.

VIVIENNE: *While speaking, pulls out ether and rubs it on her arms and
neck.* The worst thing is the air raids. Every night. Whoop, whoop,
whoop. And Tom just ignores them. Does he close the curtains?
No. I have to get out of bed, and he knows I'm not well, and I have

to close them myself so we don't go to jail. Tom doesn't like to be interrupted when he's writing. I write too, you know, Tom! And bloody well too. *Feels effects of ether, gets dreamy.*

EZRA: Which reminds me, I'm dying for . . . just a little taste, Ottoline. Yoo-hoo! *(To* ELIOT.*)* I tell you, Tom—you're the only one I know with the ability to think of anything I haven't thought of before.

ELIOT: Such as?

EZRA: It's outrageous you waste eight hours a day in a bank doing numbing, mindless, meaningless—

ELIOT: What isn't?

EZRA: What?

ELIOT: Meaningless.

EZRA: Me. You see—Me is meaning. Me is life.

ELIOT: Me forget. Me has wife. And somebody has to pay the rent. And somebody has to pay the rent.

EZRA: "Sooner murder an infant in its cradle than nurse unacted desire." Blake. Of course.

ELIOT: Blake was a bachelor.

OTTOLINE: *(To* ELIOT.*)* So was the Ripper.

ELIOT: Don't be so sure.

EZRA: *(To* OTTOLINE.*)* I'm thirsty.

Pause.

VIVIENNE: Maybe the Kaiser is Montague's son. I mean, Jack's son—

ELIOT *crosses to* VIVIENNE, *angry.* EZRA *moves in on* OTTOLINE.

OTTOLINE: —or, wait. I mean, John. *(To* EZRA.*)* Right? *(To* VIVIENNE.*)* These two insist on precision.

ELIOT: *(To* VIVIENNE.*) Grabs ether bottle.* Half-empty.

VIVIENNE: Half-full. I feel awful, you know.

ELIOT: You need sleep. Go lay down.

EZRA: *Raises glass.* I'm being ignored.

ELIOT: You're embarrassing me.

VIVIENNE: Don't touch me.

OTTOLINE: So, tell me—

ELIOT: *Walks away.* Don't talk anymore. *Aside.* Five. One, two, three, four, f—

Pause.

VIVIENNE: It was only a simple question, Tom.

ELIOT *smiles.*

EZRA: Oh, Ms. Morrell. Look—*Turns glass upside down.* Bone-dry!

ELIOT: *Turns to* VIVIENNE. Hush up. *Turns away.* Four. One, two, three, fo—

VIVIENNE: And, besides, how the hell do you know?

EZRA *and* OTTOLINE: He knows everything.

VIVIENNE: He doesn't know me. Not at all.

Silence.

OTTOLINE: Now about Jack the Ripper's—

ELIOT: He was a man. And the soul of a man lives in his son.

EZRA: If his son is alive, he'd be what? Twenty-nine?

OTTOLINE: Twenty-seven.

EZRA: Just like Tom.

ELIOT: Just like Tom.

Pause.

ELIOT *smiles.*

OTTOLINE: Oh, don't tell me—You think you're Jack's son?

EZRA: John's son.

ELIOT: Someone is. Someone knows. *Drifts.*

VIVIENNE: That's ridiculous, Tom.

OTTOLINE: If you're Jack's son, who's Tom?

EZRA: I'm too thirsty to care.

OTTOLINE: Who are you, Tom?

ELIOT: *Stands.* I am . . . the son of . . . me mum . . . *Collapses into chair laughing.*

Silence.

VIVIENNE: *(To* OTTOLINE.*)* He's tipsy.

OTTOLINE: *Fills* ELIOT's *glass.* Then he must atone.

ELIOT *drinks.*

EZRA: You're a sage. *Holds out empty glass to* ELIOT.

ELIOT: *Spit take.* Piss off.

EZRA: How 'bout a tease, for me. Please? ELIOT *pours from his glass into* EZRA's. More. More. More. ELIOT's *glass is empty.* And now . . . A toast to T. S. . . . Eliot, that is— Son of the man we call— . . .

Loud air raid siren suddenly blasts.

OTTOLINE: Son of a bitch.

VIVIENNE: Oh, no.

OTTOLINE: Air raid!

EZRA: I must finish!

OTTOLINE: Silence! I hear an announcement, I think.

Silence.

OTTOLINE *and* VIVIENNE *listen intently for planes.*

EZRA: *Announcing.* Das . . . ist . . . de Kaiser, mein freunden.

VIVIENNE: Stop it!

EZRA: Das ist alles für dat dummkopf King George. *Downs drink.*

OTTOLINE: That's not funny. Not in the least.

EZRA: My intention was—

ELIOT: Parody.

EZRA: You ought to be King!

OTTOLINE: *Suddenly.* Oh, I left the windows open. *Stands. Pretends to be jovial.* Draw the curtains. Dim the lights. *Exits.*

Pause.

VIVIENNE: I feel ill. *Starts rubbing lotion from bottle.*

EZRA: What's that?

ELIOT: Cologne.

VIVIENNE: Ether. Medication. I'm not at all well.

EZRA: May I try some?

VIVIENNE: Of course.

ELIOT: Vivien, don't you dare.

VIVIENNE: Stop it. You've no right—

ELIOT: You're sick, remember?

OTTOLINE: *Offstage.* Yoo-hoo! Herr Kaiser!

VIVIENNE: *(To* ELIOT.*)* I hate—*Rises.*

OTTOLINE: *Offstage.* Kaiser!

ELIOT: Sit down, dear.

OTTOLINE: *Offstage.* Wie gehts? LIGHTS *dim.*

VIVIENNE: I hate—

ELIOT: Sit.

EZRA: *Picks up ether, rubs it on.* This is wonderful stuff. Where'd you get it?

VIVIENNE: I'm sick! The world's sick! Oh! I hate—I hate—*Starts to exit. Grabs bottle from* EZRA. Give me this. *Storms off stage.*

OTTOLINE: *Offstage.* Das du neben eine Fraulein, mein Kaiser?

VIVIENNE: *Offstage.* Stop it! Stop it!

EZRA: What does she hate, Tom? You? Or—

OTTOLINE: *Offstage.* Ya wo.

ELIOT: It's a ruse.

OTTOLINE: *Offstage.* What's that smell?

VIVIENNE: *Offstage.* Ether. Try some.

ELIOT *shudders.* EZRA *starts to fall asleep.*

EZRA: Dear, dear. My little marsupial—Thomas—I think—

OTTOLINE: *Offstage.* This stuff is nice!

VIVIENNE: *Offstage.* Have some more.

EZRA: You, my good man, are afraid of your wife—*Snores.*

ELIOT: Vivienne?

In his sleep EZRA *transforms into* EDDY.

EDDY'S VOICE: *From* EZRA. Do her in.

ELIOT: Do I dare?

EDDY'S VOICE: *From* EZRA. Oh, why not? Here's a knife. Top left
pocket.

ELIOT: Vivienne!

BLACKOUT.

Air raid siren continues. When air raid siren stops, low light rises. EZRA *is
on floor, passed out from the ether.*

ELIOT: How should I begin?

EDDY'S VOICE: *From* EZRA. Honey, calm down.

ELIOT: Dad? Is that you? Where are you?

EDDY'S VOICE: *From* EZRA. In here.

ELIOT: Inside Ezra Pound?

EDDY'S VOICE: *From* EZRA. His head's my hotel. Nice place. Clean sheets. *Quietly.* By the way— Is he dead?

APPOLLINAIRE'S VOICE: *From* EZRA. Nothing's dead . . . —except what does not yet exist.

ELIOT: Appollinaire?

APPOLLINAIRE'S VOICE: *From* EZRA. Greetings! *Snores.*

EDDY'S VOICE: *From* EZRA. He's old. We're roommates.

ELIOT: You're joking.

APPOLLINAIRE'S VOICE: *From* EZRA. Greetings! *Snores.*

EDDY'S VOICE: *From* EZRA. Do him in, too. He's driving me nuts.

EZRA: *Wakes up suddenly.* Tom! I had a thought—

ELIOT: Good lord. *Rubs ether on* EZRA. Sorry, Pop.

EDDY'S VOICE: *From* EZRA. You know I'm allergic to ether.

EZRA *snores.*

ELIOT: He's not.

EDDY'S VOICE: *From* EZRA. Stop it! Oooh—I'm itching all over! Put that stuff away—

ELIOT: We gotta talk.

EDDY'S VOICE: *From* EZRA. I have hives on my face! Yuck! No more. I'll stay. Talk. Okay? What's up, son? Wait—don't tell me—you're gay.

ELIOT: Dad!

EDDY'S VOICE: *From* EZRA. Not so loud. I'm supposed to be dead.

ELIOT: I'm supposed to be king.

EDDY'S VOICE: *From* EZRA. Oh, that. Look, I'm sorry—I'm working on it.

ELIOT: It's been seven years, Dad.

DRUITT'S VOICE: *From* EZRA. Eddy?

EDDY'S VOICE: *From* EZRA. Oh, Lord. Druitt! How are you?

DRUITT'S VOICE: *From* EZRA. Dead. And yourself?

EDDY'S VOICE: *From* EZRA. Oh, the same. *Whispers to* ELIOT. Thomas— Help!

ELIOT: Good night, John. *Rubs ether on* EZRA.

DRUITT'S VOICE: *From* EZRA. What's that smell? Eddy! *Snores.*

EDDY'S VOICE: *From* EZRA. Thank you.

ELIOT: Tell me—how come George is still on the throne? George is a moron. This war should be over.

EDDY'S VOICE: *From* EZRA. You'll have to be patient. I'll take care of it soon.

ELIOT: People are dying—

EDDY'S VOICE: *From* EZRA. I'm dying, too.

ELIOT: Oh. I didn't know. When did this start?

EDDY'S VOICE: *From* EZRA. I started dying the day I was born.

ELIOT: You know what you are? A coward.

EDDY'S VOICE: *From* EZRA. And you?

ELIOT: I know what I'm not.

EDDY'S VOICE: *From* EZRA. You're not dead.

APPOLLINAIRE'S VOICE: *From* EZRA. Nothing's dead—

EDDY'S VOICE: *From* EZRA. Oh, shut up!

Gunshot. Silence.

ELIOT: Dad? Eddy? John?

Silence.

ELIOT: Jack?

STEPHEN WHITE'S VOICE: *From* EZRA. Hello, Thomas.

ELIOT: Who are you?

STEPHEN WHITE'S VOICE: *From* EZRA. Let's just say—I'm a friend—

ELIOT: Go away. *Rubs ether on* EZRA.

STEPHEN WHITE'S VOICE: *From* EZRA. Sorry, lad. You'll never get rid of me. I know who you are. We had a deal.

ELIOT: Stephen White?

STEPHEN WHITE'S VOICE: *From* EZRA. Very good.

ELIOT: What are you doing here?

STEPHEN WHITE'S VOICE: *From* EZRA. Making sure you remember.

ELIOT: How could I forget?

STEPHEN WHITE'S VOICE: *From* EZRA. When we drink, we get careless. When we're careless—we die.

ELIOT: I started dying the day I was born.

STEPHEN WHITE'S VOICE: *From* EZRA. The day you were born, someone murdered two whores.

ELIOT: How do you know?

STEPHEN WHITE'S VOICE: *From* EZRA. I know everything, Thomas.

ELIOT: You don't know me. Not at all.

STEPHEN WHITE'S VOICE: *From* EZRA. That's what you think. I have eyes everywhere. They're paid to watch you. You slip up just once—

ELIOT: Mum's the word.

STEPHEN WHITE'S VOICE: *From* EZRA. You've been warned.

Pause.

ELIOT: By the way—how's your wife?

STEPHEN WHITE'S VOICE: *From* EZRA. That's not funny.

ELIOT: Oh, my! Neither is this. *Puts knife to* EZRA's *throat.*

EZRA: *Waking up suddenly. Gasps.* Tom—I'm your friend!

Awkward silence.

ELIOT: Sorry, umm—

EZRA: Oh, you loon! *Laughs.* I thought it was a knife—it's only a pen! . . . My pen.

ELIOT: Fell out of your pocket. Top left.

EZRA: Have I been out long?

ELIOT: A few years.

EZRA: Anything change?

ELIOT: Everyone's dead.

EZRA: *In* APOLLINAIRE's *voice.* Nothing's dead—except—

ELIOT: Here— Have more of this . . . *Spreads ether on* EZRA. EZRA *snores.*

Fade LIGHTS. BLACKOUT.

END OF SCENE IV

SCENE V
Backstage, Near Dressing Womb
Los Angeles, 1999

WENDY'S VOICE: *On cell phone.* Stephen—calm down, do your yoga, relax— . . . As soon as Jack shows up— . . . The baby? Don't ask. He's been kicking all night. Wish you'd both go to sleep. . . . I know you're not crazy. So do the police. Okay? Me too. Bye

LIGHTS *up.* WENDY *puts cell phone away.* ANNIE *enters behind her.*

WENDY: Fucking loon.

ANNIE: Got a light?

WENDY: Do I look like I smoke?

ANNIE: I don't know.

WENDY: I'm pregnant.

ANNIE: Got a light?

WENDY: Annie? Shit—keep your head. Annie is gone. Annie is dead. WENDY *clutches her stomach.* Oww!

ANNIE: That's what the papers said.

WENDY: What's that smell?

ANNIE: Ether.

WENDY: Ha! You may hallucinate freely. JACK *kicks.* Ow! *(To womb.)* Stop it!

ANNIE: *Pulls out ether tube.* Want some ether?

WENDY: Is it bad for the—

ANNIE: Nah.

WENDY: *Rubs ether on belly.* This stuff is nice.

ANNIE: Have some more. You want Jack? Bring me Stephen White.

WENDY: I can't. He's a suspect—

ANNIE: He's a cop.

ANNIE *and* WENDY *begin to drift off stage as they do,* LIGHTS *fade up on womb.*

WENDY: *Echo voice.* Stephen? Ha! The day you died he had to hide from the cops. He hates police—thinks they're all out to get him. Since August he's been in a lunatic asylum—in New Mexico of all places—isn't that funny? *Laughs.* No cop in his right mind would look for him there. *Hysterical laughter.*

VOICE: Hurry up, please. It's time.

WENDY: *Echo voice.* Some girl.

In womb: JACK *covers his ears and kicks the walls, as* WENDY *and* ANNIE'*s echo voices continue.*

ANNIE: *Echo voice. Voice fades.* He'll be here. You'll see . . .

JACK: *Kicking.* Quiet! I'm trying to think.

LIGHTS *off on* WENDY. *Silence. TV on.* JACK *flips channels. All channels feature breaking news reports with images of the missing Jack the Rapper.*

JACK: That's me . . . that's me . . . that's me . . . what's this?—

Fade LIGHTS *on womb.*

INTERLUDE
Video

SHOT 1: Sixties protest.

SHOT 2: Armed struggle somewhere.

SHOT 3: Washington DC.

SHOT 4–10: Traffic, pollution, homeless people, sad children, etc.

V.O. (SHOTS 1–10): After all the rebellion, has anything really changed?

SHOT 11: (*From the movie* Network) I asked—Why me? And the voice said, "Because you're on television, dummy." *Freeze frame.*

V.O.: Welcome to "This Time, the Revolution Will Be Televised." Sponsored by:

SHOT 12: List of thousands of names, all indiscernible.

V.O.: Tonight's special guest . . .

Fade TV. Raise LIGHTS *on womb.*

JACK: Me.

V.O.: The madman—J.C.

JACK *watches, nonplussed. Enter* ANNIE.

ANNIE: Hi, Jack.

JACK *leaps up and turns around.*

JACK: Devil woman.

ANNIE: How you been?

JACK: Go away.

ANNIE: Ready yet?

JACK: Not on your life.

ANNIE: Ah, my friend, you do not know, you do not know what life is, you who hold it in your hands.

JACK: Get out.

ANNIE: Everyone thought we would be such good friends.

JACK: We're not.

SOUND: *Cell phone ring echoes.*

WENDY: *Echo voice. (To cell phone.)* This is Knight.

ANNIE: Not yet.

WENDY: *Echo voice. (To cell phone.)* Stephen who? Stephen White?

JACK: What's that smell?

ANNIE: Medication.

WENDY: *Echo voice.* You sound weird.

JACK: Smells like ether.

WENDY: *Echo voice.* This is not Stephen White.

JACK: I'm allergic to ether. It's making me itch. *Scratches.*

WENDY: *Echo voice.* How dare you—Shit.

JACK *kicks.*

ANNIE: Uh-oh. I see hives. Let's go—

JACK: *Stops scratching.* Nice try.

WENDY: *Echo voice. On cell phone.* Stephen, it's me—Pick up the phone . . .

ANNIE: I like you—

WENDY: *Echo voice.* You there? . . .

ANNIE: Remember that.

WENDY: *Echo voice.* Steve! Thank God—

JACK: I like being alone . . .

WENDY: *Echo voice.* listen— . . .

JACK: with all the—

WENDY: *Echo voice.* What?

JACK: —old nocturnal smells. Smells—

WENDY: *Echo voice.* Who is this!

JACK: —of chestnuts in the street—and female—

WENDY: *Echo voice.* Ann who?

JACK: —smells in shuttered rooms—

WENDY: *Echo voice.* Ann D.?

JACK: —and cigarettes in corridors—

ANNIE: You do not know me. *Exits.*

WENDY: *Echo voice.* Annie!

JACK: and cocktail smells in bars . . . in bars . . . in bars . . . in bars . . .

Fade LIGHTS *to black.*

END OF SCENE V

SCENE VI—PART I
Inside Pub
Whitechapel, London, 1888
Half-past three

In BLACKOUT, STEPHEN WHITE *reads unfinished letter that* EDDY *was writing at the bar before he stepped outside to urinate.*

STEPHEN WHITE'S VOICE: *Reads.* Dear Boss, I keep on hearing the police have caught me but they won't fix me just yet. I have laughed when they look so clever and talk about being on the right track. I am down on whores and shan't quit ripping them till I do get buckled. *Speaks.* Buckled? I like that. Eddy—you're a sage. Buckled. Meaning . . . hmm . . . What else?

LIGHTS *up.* STEPHEN WHITE *continues to read letter at bar.*

STEPHEN WHITE: Grand work the last job was. I gave the lady no time to squeal. *Pause. Speaks.* That's true. *Reads.* I saved some of the proper red stuff in a ginger beer bottle— *Speaks.* Nice touch. *Reads.* Red ink is fit enough I hope ha ha.—

CATHERINE: *Offstage.* Flowers!

STEPHEN WHITE: Stall him. *Yells pre-established code to* CATHERINE. Curse it! *Pause.* Good. *Reads.* My knife is nice and sharp. I love my work— Etcetera. Etcetera. Good luck. . . . Yours truly, Jack the Ripper. *Speaks.* Jack the Ripper—. . . *Laughs.* Who wrote this? *Reads.* P.S.—Don't mind me giving the trade name—

CATHERINE: *Offstage.* Flowers! A rose for ye sor? Ooooooo— . . . Is that Collars and Cuffs? Aye—It is! Eddy! Pissin', are ye? With a pen in yer hand? And no paper, I see—well, lucky for ye—I've some paper—I make paper roses, ye know. Would ye care fer a piece—eh, Ed?

DRUITT: *Offstage.* Leave me be—

CATHERINE: *Offstage.* Ooo . . . Lookie there, Eddy . . . I see yer winkie!

STEPHEN WHITE: *Still at bar.* I think this letter could use a bit more. Let's see— . . . Aye, I like it. Wait. *Picks up pen. Writes, reads.* P.S.S. So the say I'm a doctor now—ha ha. *Speaks.* Still want to play games, Eddy? You lose. Ha-Ha!

Fade LIGHTS.

CATHERINE: *Offstage.* Night, Eddy. Flowers! Roses!

Enter DRUITT. *Sees note. Looks worried. Rushes out.*

BLACKOUT. *Begin* AUDIO.

SCENE VI—PART II
Later, Inside Same Pub

EDDY'S VOICE: *Reads.* So they say I'm a doctor now. Ha ha. *Speaks.* Ha ha? *Yells.* Montague—what's the meaning of this?

DRUITT'S VOICE: Rotten cop . . . Must have been—yes, that's it—when I went out to piss—The postcard was in my pocket, I thought. I came back in the pub and—

LIGHTS *up.*

DRUITT: White was gone. I'll wager he wrote it. The bastard—

EDDY: Druitt— . . . You left the pub?

DRUITT: 'Ad to. You know 'ow it is. . . . When a man has to piss—

EDDY: Are you out of your mind?

DRUITT: I was there 'alf the night—

EDDY: 'Alf the night?

DRUITT: 'Alf the night.

EDDY: Drunk were you, then?

DRUITT: I only 'ad tea. Twenty-two cups and still White wouldn't leave. After writing yours truly, J—I felt me 'ead roll. I think to meself—me tea 'as been drooged. I left an' I retched. I did 'ave a piss. I was gone but a minute—I come back, I see this.

EDDY: In a minute there is time for decisions and revisions which a minute will reverse. . . . *Thoughtful.* Do I dare— . . . disturb the universe? *Silly.* Oh, why not. *(To* DRUITT.*)* Get a knife.

DRUITT: A what?

EDDY: A knife. Get it. *Pause.* Annie . . . forgive me. I have to do this. *Starts writing.* Wasn't good . . . enough to post . . . this before I got . . . all the red ink—*(To* DRUITT.*)* Where's the knife? *Writing*— . . . off my hands.

DRUITT: Curse it.

EDDY: *Writing.* Curse it.

DRUITT: I'm sorry.

EDDY: Too late. Done.

DRUITT: I did my best.

EDDY: Mail this. But first—Give me your hand. This is for pissing. This is for me. *Cuts* DRUITT's *hand.* DRUITT *shouts.* This is for Anne.

DRUITT: She read the papers? I'll send it to *The Times.*

Exits. Leaves letter on bar.

The letter traverses time. MARY JANE *appears. Picks up note—passes it to* OTTOLINE—*who passes it to* STEPHEN *in med gown.*

SCENE VI—PART III
Mental Asylum
New Mexico, 1999

STEPHEN *and the voices in his head.*

STEPHEN: *Reading letter.* Yours truly, Jack the Ripper—Rapper—
Where's my cell phone? Where's my cell phone? I gotta have my
cell phone!

STEPHEN WHITE: I never had a cell phone. Why should you have one?

STEPHEN: Times change.

STEPHEN WHITE: You changed, my friend. You've changed. You've
become a Hollow Man.

STEPHEN: Don't tell me Wendy signed that band?

STEPHEN WHITE: A Hollow Man is not a band.—

STEPHEN: Listen, man. I'm in the business, see?

STEPHEN WHITE: Not recently.

STEPHEN: I've been on vacation, but—

STEPHEN WHITE: You've been hiding.

STEPHEN: Did she tell you that?

STEPHEN WHITE: No, Stephen—

STEPHEN: *Gulps.* You know me?

STEPHEN WHITE: What's to know, Hollow Man? You are empty.

STEPHEN: I'm a musician at heart.

STEPHEN WHITE: You're a dick and a car.

STEPHEN: How is my car?

STEPHEN WHITE: It's not yours anymore. Since you murdered that whore—

STEPHEN: I didn't kill her.

STEPHEN WHITE: Who did?

STEPHEN: Jack the Rapper.

STEPHEN WHITE: Jack the Rapper is you.

Pause.

STEPHEN: Prove it.

STEPHEN WHITE: It's true. The police say it's true. And the press, and the president—

STEPHEN: I'm a scapegoat for someone—

STEPHEN WHITE: The question is who.

Pause.

STEPHEN: Speaking of who—what's your name, pal?

STEPHEN WHITE: Stephen. Stephen White. Like you. Just like you. I'm you tonight. A musician—

STEPHEN: You play? Get your axe, man—we'll jam—

STEPHEN WHITE: Steve—

STEPHEN: Stephen—

STEPHEN WHITE: I'll call you whatever I damn—well, please—killer, coward, Jack the Rapper, arse, cop— . . .

Pause.

STEPHEN: Don't call me cop.

STEPHEN WHITE: I'm a cop.

STEPHEN: No you're not. If you were, you'd arrest me. Ha!

STEPHEN WHITE: Why give you credit? I'm Steven White.

STEPHEN: Me too.

STEPHEN WHITE: Not tonight. You ripped me off. I should sue you. You blew it. I'm Jack the Ripper.

DRUITT: Fuck you.

STEPHEN WHITE: Is that Druitt or Eddy?

DRUITT: Neither. I'm . . . ummm . . . Where's my passport? I'm . . . umm . . . Leon Beron! A Russian Jew, from France.

STEPHEN WHITE: You were killed in 1910.

ELIOT: New Year's Day, 1911.

DRUITT: Eliot?

STEPHEN WHITE: We had a deal.

ELIOT: The deal is off.

DRUITT: I'm dead?

STEPHEN WHITE: Oh, no!

APPOLLINAIRE: Greetings! Nothing's dead. *Continue over* EZRA. Except for what does not yet exist.

EZRA: Appollinaire.

APPOLLINAIRE: Greetings!

EZRA: I'm Ezra.

OTTOLINE: Ezra? Ezra Pound?

EZRA: In the flesh— . . . Ottoline, dear. Where's my check?

STEPHEN: I found my cell phone!

OTTOLINE: Pound—You're dead.

ELIOT: No!

APPOLLINAIRE: Nothing's dead—Except—That which does not yet exist.

STEPHEN: Get out of this hotel. Get out! *Dials cell phone.*

WENDY'S VOICE: *Over cell phone.* This is Knight.

STEPHEN: Wendy. Stephen.

WENDY'S VOICE: *Over cell phone.* Stephen who?

STEPHEN: Stephen White!

WENDY'S VOICE: *Over cell phone.* Stephen White?

STEPHEN: You double crosser—*Chokes.*

WENDY'S VOICE: *Over cell phone.* You sound weird.

STEPHEN WHITE: I can smell you from here.

WENDY'S VOICE: *Over cell phone.* This is not Stephen White.

STEPHEN WHITE: I'll murder you—

WENDY'S VOICE: *Over cell phone.* How dare you. *Hangs up.*

STEPHEN WHITE: She is alone.

Silence.

Cell phone rings.

WENDY'S VOICE: *Over cell phone answering machine.* Stephen, it's me. Pick up the phone. Stephen, you there?

STEPHEN WHITE: Answer it, Stephen.

STEPHEN: Hello?

WENDY'S VOICE: *Over cell phone.* Stephen, thank God, listen—

STEPHEN: Wendy, help! *Chokes, dies.*

WENDY'S VOICE: *Over cell phone.* What?

STEPHEN WHITE: Hello, dear.

WENDY'S VOICE: *Over cell phone.* Who is this? Where's Steve?

STEPHEN WHITE: Where's Anne?

WENDY'S VOICE: *Over cell phone.* Who's Ann?

STEPHEN WHITE: Anne D—

WENDY'S VOICE: *Over cell phone.* Anne D—?

STEPHEN WHITE: You know who I mean.

BLACKOUT.

END OF SCENE VI

INTERLUDE
Video
Los Angeles, 1999

HIP TV REPORTER IN STUDIO: Is Jack the Rapper just a hoax? Is he dead? Nobody knows. Reporter Colin Wilson is in LA, where he says the fans are growing restless—Colin, tell us—what's the latest.

TV on.

REPORTER COLIN WILSON: It's four o'clock here in LA. Officially the show is on. But after waiting for so long, for the star to appear, many fans fear the Rapper is— The rumor most believe is that Jack rests in peace.

VIDEO GIRL GROUPIE: He can't be dead! He can't be dead! You know what I paid for these tickets? *Cries.*

VIDEO ROCK DUDE: I'm wasted.

VIDEO ROCK CHICK: Wow.

VIDEO GOTH GIRL: He's dead? That's cool.

VIDEO GOTH GUY: Right on. Me too. *Drops dead.*

FOUR SUITS ON CELL PHONES: I'm here. Where are you?

FRAT BOY: Total rip off.

ROCK DUDE: Dude, like I'm so wasted.

SILLY GIRL: Jack who?

COLIN WILSON: As you can see, reactions here, live at the Jack the Rapper show, are mixed. The truth is the story is not over yet. As we wait for the end, the beginning remains.

SCENE VII
Home in St. Louis, Missouri, 1910
Four o'clock

ANNIE DUNNE, *alone in room.*

ANNIE DUNNE: *Sings.* It was only a violet I plucked from my mother's grave as a boy . . . *Hums.*

LIGHTS *fade up slowly.* ANNIE DUNNE *holds a faded letter in her hands.*

The past is like a song to me, a melody with words. The past cannot be undone, even if it is unknown. Yet . . . if the past remains unknown, the present is affected. For the present is the past. And the song must be remembered.

Enter ELIOT.

ELIOT: Ah, my dear Annie Dunne, love of my life. The world's greatest nannie, a marvelous cook! I shall miss you terrifically when I move across the sea.

ANNIE DUNNE: Tom, dear. . . . umm . . . we need to talk. Before you go away forever. There's something you need to know.

ELIOT: No time like the present. *Sits.* Let's talk.

ANNIE DUNNE: You've known me all your life. I was there from the beginning, was I not?

ELIOT: Of course! And I shall never forget all you have done for me. Raising me even more so than Mother. What is this about?

ANNIE DUNNE: But do you really know who I am?

ELIOT: A true living saint!

ANNIE DUNNE: I am . . . A. Crook.

ELIOT: Ha! With your face? The face of an angel . . . .

Silence.

ANNIE DUNNE: You're a crook too. Half a Crook.

ELIOT: I don't know what you mean.

ANNIE DUNNE: How should I begin? The end. Yes. In my beginning is my end. At least to you it is. *Pause.* Read this. *Hands letter to* TOM.

ELIOT: *Reads.* "Since Friday I felt I was going to be like mother, and the best thing for me was to die." What does this mean?

ANNIE DUNNE: It was written by a dear friend of mine. A man— Eddy. Well, he used to be Eddy. He used to be a lot of things. Your . . .

ELIOT: Is he dead?

ANNIE DUNNE: I thought he was. I've wasted my life for twenty-two years.

ELIOT: Hey, now. That's how long you've been taking care of me! I wouldn't call that a waste.

ANNIE DUNNE: Today I received a letter from him. And I know now what he meant me to tell you. You see . . . the man who wrote that letter was a duke. And . . .

ELIOT: Oh, do tell.

ANNIE DUNNE: How should I begin? We were . . . he was . . . married, to me. *Pause.* Me and Eddy. The Duke and his wife. We had one rule between us—never ask why. We soared, me and Eddy. We soared. We were spirits. You don't know. You do not know. . . . Our enemies hated us. We were married in secret. We had other secrets. To keep them—we shared them—in bits and pieces. We'd chop up our secrets and spread them around. We considered it art. We used people like paint. It was fun for a while. Then horrid.

Pause.

ANNIE DUNNE: I wasn't Ann Dunne, then. I was A Crook. Anne Elizabeth Crook, to the Duke. We were married in secret. We had a son. If our enemies found out about him, they would — . . . We used our art to protect him. We said our son was a daughter. No one knew.

But something went wrong. Someone found out—or suspected— and so we said our daughter was dead. . . . And even that was not enough.

Again there was doubt. Suspicions aroused. Our enemies had to have proof. I had a doctor remove a bone. I sent it to them . . . without telling Eddy. And then I ran away with the dead daughter. But the daughter was not dead. And the daughter was not a daughter. See—that bone I sent our enemies was removed from Eddy's son. And his son was not dead. And the doctor was . . . I— . . .

ELIOT: *Coldly.* A rib bone?

ANNIE DUNNE: Yes.

ELIOT: You see this? *Pulls up shirt. Reveals metal truss around his ribcage.* A truss. You know what it does? It smells. It stinks. It rusts. It hurts. And I have to wear it. Or else—Curse it. Double hernia . . . that's what mother told everyone. That's what she told me.

ANNIE DUNNE: No, I didn't.

ELIOT: No, mother said—

ANNIE DUNNE: I'm your— . . .

Long pause.

ELIOT: You're crazy.

ANNIE DUNNE: This is the letter I received today. *Hands letter to* ELIOT.

ELIOT: *Reads.* "Dear Ann—Eddy is waiting—Is T.S. ready? Yours Truly, Eddy. P.S. Hurry up, please. It's time."

ANNIE DUNNE: King Edward VII died today. May 6, 1910. It's be in the paper tomorrow.

ELIOT: How do you know?

ANNIE DUNNE: I know. You see—Eddy planned this. To get even with someone who . . . turned art into horror. *Pause.* You are the heir to Edward VII. The problem is . . .

ELIOT: You said I was a daughter.

ANNIE DUNNE: Everyone thinks you are dead.

ELIOT: Except you.

ANNIE DUNNE: Ann Crook was once my name, now it is not. Mary Jane was a crook and Ann Crook was not. Mary Jane's alias is Kelly to some. Ann Crook's alias is Annie Dunne. Ann Crook was Eddy's wife. Mary Jane wasn't.

ELIOT: What about Eddy.

ANNIE DUNNE: They think he's dead, too. He thought it would be . . . the best thing for you. Only two people out there know who you are. If one of them finds you, he'll kill you for sure. The other one owes his life to Eddy.

ELIOT: What's his name?

ANNIE DUNNE: Used to be Montague John . . . uh—Druitt. Now it's Leon Beron.

ELIOT: Druitt, Druitt . . . I've heard that name. Wait—wasn't he Jack the Ripper?

ANNIE DUNNE: That's was you're supposed to think.

ELIOT: You know who the Ripper really is?

ANNIE DUNNE: I almost married him. See, he looked just like Eddy. And sometimes he was—like me and my sister. We used to switch roles. If I'd married John you'd have been the Ripper's son. But . . . what am I saying? Jack wasn't John.

ELIOT: Was Eddy?

ANNIE DUNNE: Tom! How dare you! Of course, I can't expect you to know. The lie lingers on. Like a song. Like a song. Everyone knows the melody, few know the words. The question is—do you dare—disturb the universe?

ELIOT: If I believe you, my whole life has become a lie . . . in a minute.

ANNIE DUNNE: In a minute there is time for decisions and revisions which a minute will reverse.

ELIOT: Do I dare?

ANNIE DUNNE: *Hands knife to* ELIOT. This is yours.

ELIOT: What is this?

ANNIE DUNNE: It's not just any knife. It belongs to Stephen White. Eddy sent it. With best regards. Go see Druitt. Or rather—see Leon Beron. He lives in Whitechapel. Beron is his name nowadays. Tell him Eddy sent you. He'll know what that means. If he refuses to say anything— . . . tell him to remember: You have the key. The key's memory.

ELIOT: Memory! How can you have memory when your past has been erased?

ANNIE DUNNE: Everything in your past was to prepare you for this.

LIGHTS *fade to* BLACKOUT.

END OF SCENE VII

SCENE VIII
Backstage, Near the Dressing Womb
Los Angeles, 1999
Four o'clock

ANNIE: *Inside womb with* JACK. The soul of a father lives in his son.

VOICE: Hurry up, please. It's time.

JACK: I'm the son me mum. *Laughs.*

ANNIE: I'm your mum. Do me in.

JACK: Do I dare?

ANNIE: Oh, why not? You've done it before.

JACK: I can't talk about that.

BLACKOUT.

LIGHTS *up on* WENDY *backstage. Enter* STEPHEN WHITE.

STEPHEN WHITE: Where is he?

WENDY: Goddamnit. You're supposed to be hiding.

STEPHEN WHITE: I'm supposed to be dead.

EZRA'S VOICE: *From inside* STEPHEN WHITE's *head.* Nothing's dead—

OTTOLINE'S VOICE: *From inside* WENDY's *head.* Ezra—is that you? Where's Eliot?

LIGHTS *up on dressing womb and backstage.*

VIVIENNE'S VOICE: *From inside* ANNIE'S *head.* Coming.

OTTOLINE'S VOICE: *From inside* WENDY'S *head.* Whose son is he now?

STEPHEN WHITE: Get out of my head. Get out!

WENDY: Umm . . . Stephen . . . —my water just broke.

STEPHEN'S VOICE: *From inside* STEPHEN WHITE'S *head.* Holy cow.

ANNIE: *(To* JACK.*)* Here's a knife. Take it.

JACK: That's a pen.

ANNIE: Oops. I took it from him—

JACK: Who?

ANNIE: Your father.

WENDY: The whole thing's a disaster. *Pushes.* Look, Stephen— *Pushes*—do me a favor, all right?— Go out there and tell everyone the show's over—*Pushes.* Jack's in here. Christ! This is the end of the world.

JACK: You fink! Annie!

ANNIE: You have the key. Do it. Me first. I'm your mum.

JACK: Who's my dad?

ANNIE: T. S. Eliot.

JACK: She thinks it's him.

ANNIE: I switched the sperm.

STEPHEN WHITE: Here comes papa! Ha-ha! Ha-ha!

WENDY: Stephen—don't touch me. Stephen—go away!

ANNIE: Do me in!

JACK: I have to use words—

ANNIE: Hurry up, please!

WENDY: It's time!

JACK: This is the way the world ends. *Draws a T on* ANNIE's *forehead.* This is the way the world ends. *Draws an S on* ANNIE's *forehead.*

STEPHEN WHITE: This is the way the world ends. *Snaps* JACK *from womb. Loud bang. Umbilical cord comes out with nothing attached.*

JACK: Not with a bang . . .

Fade LIGHTS.

ANNIE, WENDY, STEPHEN WHITE *slowly fall to ground.*

JACK *picks up paper rose.*

JACK: . . . but a whimper . . .

THE END

About the Author

KAT GEORGES IS A POET, playwright, performer, and graphic designer. She is the author of fifteen plays, including *Paglia in Persona: A Deconstruction of Camille Paglia, Arousal: An Examination of Presidential Legacy,* and *976-POWER: A Corporate Primal Scream.* Her poetry books include *Our Lady of the Hunger, Punk Rock Journal,* and *Slow Dance at 120 Beats per Minute.* Her poetry and prose work has appeared in *The San Francisco Chronicle, The Outlaw Bible of American Poetry,* and numerous regional and international journals and magazines.

In 1982, she co-founded and edited the Orange County, California punk rock magazine *The Eye* and in 1991 cofounded and edited the San Francisco poetry journal *The Fold.* Since 1988, she has edited numerous anthologies including *The Verdict Is In,* a poetic response to the 1992 Los Angeles riots (Manic D Press, San Francisco, 1993), *Along the Fault,* a collection of poems from the fledgling Los Angeles spoken word movement (Resident Alien Press, Los Angeles, 1990), and *A Gathering of the Tribes: Issue 13* (A Gathering of the Tribes, New York, 2012).

Born in Lynwood, California, raised in Long Beach and Orange County, she relocated to San Francisco in 1990, where, in 1992 she founded Marilyn Monroe Memorial Theater, a space dedicated to presenting "demolished texts, deconstructed classics, and new works." From 1992 through 2000, she and co-director Peter Carlaftes lived in, wrote, directed, and produced twenty-five original plays, and presented numerous poetry and spoken word events, sketch comedy nights, underground film events, and Dada performance gatherings. In New York since 2003, she has directed numerous Off-Broadway plays, produced more than five-hundred poetry and performance events, and performed her poetry widely. She has also performed internationally in museums, theaters, planetariums, and on the streets of London, Paris, Brussels, Rome, Berlin, Athens, and Bastia.

Currently, Georges is co-director and artistic director of the publishing company she and Carlaftes founded in 1993, Three Rooms Press: a fiercely independent press inspired by Dada, punk, and passion. She is co-editor of the annual *Maintenant: A Journal of Contemporary Dada Writing and Art,* and co-edited three editions of the mystery anthology series *Have a NYC.* She lives in New York City.

Recent and Forthcoming Books from Three Rooms Press

FICTION

Meagan Drothers
Weird Girl and What's His Name

Ron Dakron
Hello Devilfish!

Michael T. Fournier
Hidden Wheel
Swing State

Janet Hamill
Tales from the Eternal Café

William Least Heat-Moon
Celestial Mechanics

Aimee Herman
Everything Grows

Eamon Loingsigh
Light of the Diddicoy
Exile on Bridge Street

John Marshall
The Greenfather

Aram Saroyan
Still Night in L.A.

Richard Vetere
The Writers Afterlife
Champagne and Cocaine

Julia Watts
Quiver

SHORT STORY ANTHOLOGIES

Dark City Lights: New York Stories
edited by Lawrence Block

First-Person Singularities: Stories
by Robert Silverberg
with an introduction by John Scalzi

Have a NYC I, II & III:
New York Short Stories;
edited by Peter Carlaftes
& Kat Georges

Crime + Music: The Sounds of Noir
edited by Jim Fusilli

Songs of My Selfie:
An Anthology of Millennial Stories
edited by Constance Renfrow

The Obama Inheritance:
15 Stories of Conspiracy Noir
edited by Gary Phillips

This Way to the End Times:
Classic and New Stories of
the Apocalypse
edited by Robert Silverberg

MEMOIR & BIOGRAPHY

Nassrine Azimi and
Michel Wasserman
Last Boat to Yokohama:
The Life and Legacy of
Beate Sirota Gordon

William S. Burroughs & Allen Ginsberg
Don't Hide the Madness:
William S. Burroughs in Conversation
with Allen Ginsberg
edited by Steven Taylor

James Carr
BAD: The Autobiography of
James Carr

Richard Katrovas
Raising Girls in Bohemia:
Meditations of an American Father; A
Memoir in Essays

Judith Malina
Full Moon Stages:
Personal Notes from
50 Years of The Living Theatre

Phil Marcade
Punk Avenue:
Inside the New York City
Underground, 1972-1982

Stephen Spotte
My Watery Self:
Memoirs of a Marine Scientist

PHOTOGRAPHY-MEMOIR

Mike Watt
On & Off Bass

MIXED MEDIA

John S. Paul
Sign Language: A Painter's Notebook
(photography, poetry and prose)

FILM & PLAYS

Israel Horovitz
My Old Lady: Complete Stage Play
and Screenplay with an Essay on
Adaptation

Peter Carlaftes
Triumph For Rent (3 Plays)
Teatrophy (3 More Plays)

Kat Georges
Three Somebodies: Plays about
Notorious Dissidents

DADA

Maintenant: A Journal of
Contemporary Dada Writing & Art
(Annual, since 2008)

TRANSLATIONS

Thomas Bernhard
On Earth and in Hell
(poems of Thomas Bernhard
with English translations by
Peter Waugh)

Patrizia Gattaceca
Isula d'Anima / Soul Island
(poems by the author
in Corsican with English
translations)

César Vallejo | Gerard Malanga
Malanga Chasing Vallejo
(selected poems of César Vallejo
with English translations
and additional notes by
Gerard Malanga)

George Wallace
EOS: Abductor of Men
(selected poems in Greek & English)

POETRY COLLECTIONS

Hala Alyan
Atrium

Peter Carlaftes
DrunkYard Dog
I Fold with the Hand I Was Dealt

Thomas Fucaloro
It Starts from the Belly and Blooms
Inheriting Craziness is Like
a Soft Halo of Light

Kat Georges
Our Lady of the Hunger

Robert Gibbons
Close to the Tree

Israel Horovitz
Heaven and Other Poems

David Lawton
Sharp Blue Stream

Jane LeCroy
Signature Play

Philip Meersman
This is Belgian Chocolate

Jane Ormerod
Recreational Vehicles on Fire
Welcome to the Museum of Cattle

Lisa Panepinto
On This Borrowed Bike

George Wallace
Poppin' Johnny

HUMOR

Peter Carlaftes
A Year on Facebook

Three Rooms Press | New York, NY | Current Catalog: www.threeroomspress.com
Three Rooms Press books are distributed by PGW/Ingram: www.pgw.com

CPSIA information can be obtained
at www.ICGtesting.com
Printed in the USA
LVHW01s0109140218
566484LV00002B/2/P